Gender, Aging and the State

Gender, Aging and the State

Edited by
Barbara Nichols and Peter Leonard

Third in the series of monographs, School of Social Work, McGill University.

BLACK ROSE BOOKS

Montréal/New York
London

BLACK ROSE BOOKS No. X212
Hardcover 1-895431-97-2
Paperback1-895431-96-4

Library of Congress No. 94-71246

Canadian Cataloguing in Publication Data

Main entry under title:
Gender, aging and the state

Includes bibliographical references
ISBN 1-895431-97-2 (bound) –
ISBN 1-895431-96-4 (pbk.)

1. Aged women — Social conditions. 2. Aging.
I. Nichols, Barbara II. Leonard, Peter

HQ1233.G46 1994 305.26 C94-900190-2

The article "Old Women's Experiences of Needing Care: Choice or Compulsion,"
by Jane Aronson was previously published in the *Canadian Journal on Aging*.

Mailing Address

BLACK ROSE BOOKS
C.P. 1258
Succ. Place du Parc
Montréal, Québec
H2W 2R3 Canada

BLACK ROSE BOOKS
340 Nagel Drive
Cheektowaga, New York
14225 USA

Printed in Canada

A publication of the Institute of Policy Alternatives of Montréal
(IPAM)

Contents

Contributors

Jane Aronson is associate professor at the School of Social Work, McMaster University. She is currently engaged in research on women's work as paid and unpaid carers, and on shifting images of families.

Frances Barskey is a retired teacher and member of the *Voice of Women* in Montréal.

Marilyn Bicher is a sociologist and social worker teaching at Vanier College, Montréal where she is co-ordinator of the Department of Social and Cultural Sciences. She is a researcher and member of the Montreal Health Press.

Rita Bonar teaches gerontology at Vanier College, Montréal and aging and ethnicity at Université de Montréal. She is currently undertaking a research project on community centres and long-term care facilities.

Nancy Houlahan is a graduate of the McGill Master of Social Work programme and presently employed in the Department of Social Work at the Royal Victoria Hospital, Montréal.

Peter Leonard is professor and former director of the McGill School of Social Work and past president of the Canadian Association of Schools of Social Work. Research interests include postmodern perspectives on social welfare.

Michael MacLean is professor of gerontology and social work at McMaster University and president of the Canadian Association on Gerontology.

Barbara Nichols is associate professor at the McGill School of Social Work and is currently engaged in research on women refugees.

David Woodsworth is professor emeritus and former director of the McGill School of Social Work and a member of the NDG Senior Citizens Council, Montréal.

The Theory and Politics of Aging

Peter Leonard and Barbara Nichols

This book explores a set of relationships of crucial importance to social welfare in Western countries, namely those between gender, aging and the State. These relationships are complex and often contradictory, not least because they involve three different kinds of phenomena: a social and sexual division (gender), a social and biological process (aging), and a set of political institutions (the State). Current discourse on these phenomena and their relationships with each other reveals major theoretical divergence which has resulted in a number of questions of considerable importance for the fields of social policy and social work. Is gender the central social division around which analysis, practice and political struggle should take place? Should it take priority in our thinking and action over class divisions, historically seen as the most significant, or over ethnic and racial divisions, now seen by many as more important? If gender, race, and class are alternately of equal or parallel significance, how are we to understand *their* relationship to each other?

The impact of gender, class, and ethnicity on the experience of aging and on the social position of older people is the focus of the essays in this book. It is a subject matter which is, however, located within another set of debates. In the work being undertaken to show that the experience of aging is socially constructed by the relationships and structures in which it occurs, what understanding should we have of the undeniably physical base of growing older? In the case of aging, as with gender, while we can distinguish between biological factors and the social inequalities that are often legitimated by reference to those factors, we still need to acknowledge the irreducible materiality of human life. This materiality involves anticipating the end of our physical beings, an anticipation which we may assume affects all social relationships that construct the experience of aging. How can this anticipation be taken into account without embracing the now widely-discredited notion of disengagement as a crucial process in old age?

To say that the State itself is historically constructed and reproduced within the relations of gender, class and ethnicity, and that this historically specific context determines the political response to old age leaves open a large number of questions.

For those actively engaged in the development of social policy and the practice of social work, perhaps the most important question is that concerning the place of human intention, resistance and struggle within and against the massive social forces—economic, cultural and political—to which we are all subject in modern or postmodern societies. The question regarding the effects of human intention is essentially about whether we are subjects in the two different senses of the word. We are certainly subjected to the social structure in which we live; constructed and perhaps determined by it. But are we also individual subjects in the humanist sense, and so, still able to *act upon* the world on the basis of our intentions, as well as being acted upon? This question is central in contemporary social theory, and its answers are what separate humanists from antihumanists, critical theorists from structuralists and poststructuralists, and those who believe in progress from their postmodernist critics.

The questions that we have posed here in our introduction, such as the relation between gender, class, ethnicity and the State in the social construction of aging; the significance of the biological basis of aging; and the interaction between intention and a determining environment in the experiences and consciousness of older people—are, we believe, of such importance that they deserve some extended discussion.

All of the essays in this book make reference to a precise sociocultural location of a specific population of older people. Jane Aronson, Marilyn Bicher, Michael MacLean, Nancy Houlahan, and Frances Barskey all render an account of the experiences of elderly, white middle-class women. In contrast, Rita Bonar explores the situations and reflections of ethnic minority Italian working-class women, and David Woodsworth's essay is a commentary on aging by a middle-class white male.

Reading these essays provides evidence of the importance of resisting any theoretical and political tendency to treat the categories of gender, class and ethnicity in a universal and homogeneous manner. It is clear to us that not only is the experience of aging a diverse one, but that this diversity is in each case a product of a specific set of interactions of gender, class and ethnicity. We can no more make satisfactory generalizations about *women's* experience of aging, for example, than we can about aging as a *class* phenomenon, or as an *ethnic* experience. Aging is socially constructed in such a complex way that no *a priori* preference can be given to either gender, or class, or ethnicity as a primary social category. While it may be politically important at a given historical juncture for feminists, or socialists, or anti-racists to argue for the priority of the social division with which each is most closely identified through struggle, these priorities essentially reflect strategic and tactical considerations. The major universal categories which have emerged historically from participation in political struggle against diverse forms of oppression—women, the working class, ethnic minorities—must be deconstructed if we are to give an account of the particular oppressions and opportunities experienced by specific populations of older people. We should perhaps conceive of these populations in hyphenated terms in order to understand the experience of aging of Afro-Canadian working-class men, or white Latin-American-immigrant middle-class women, for example. Whether common experiences of poverty, or gender, or ethnic minority status are strong enough to suggest a common struggle in relation to State policies and services is a political issue concerning the possibilities of alliances and coali-

4

tions—a question we will pursue later in this introductory essay.

The experience of aging is not, however, constructed only within the major social divisions of gender, class and ethnicity and their relationship to the State. It is also physiologically constructed. Of course, the physical experiences of aging, the experiences of health and ill-health, of biological deterioration and decline, are experienced within the context of State services, neighbourhood networks and the caregiving capacities of families. So, the health of older people has significant structural determinants, but is nevertheless irreducibly biological. Later, this essay will focus on inadequate material circumstances—the poverty and the physical experience of lack of resources of many elderly people—but here, we must acknowledge the biological basis of aging. Intimations of physical deterioration and pain experienced by the older women who speak to us in this book, especially in the essays by Aronson, Bicher, and Bonar, and their resulting fear of dependency and loneliness, are moving in their challenge to us to confront the reality of dying and death. Some of the voices manage to maintain a life-affirming optimism, an optimism that we see in even the very old who speak to us in MacLean, Houlahan and Barskey's study, and in Woodsworth's eloquently expressed joy at the freedom which comes to him with being "an old man." What is clearly acknowledged throughout this book, however, is that we are biological beings as well as social beings. While we try to reconstruct the social world according to our socialist and feminist aims into one of social justice and nonsexist emancipation, we cannot lose sight of our finite biological nature. The inexorable approach of deterioration and death, the final triumph of our biological over our social being is, for some, an anticipation filled with fear and despondency—depression is an ever-present risk of old age. But biological determinism, in the last instance, need not be accompanied by a parallel structural determinism of a narrow mechanistic kind: the possibility of individual intentions counting for something in old age is strongly asserted in parts of this book. If we can't be optimistic in the face of death, can we perhaps be optimistic about the opportunity to resist the more oppressive features of the *social* construction of aging?

The essay by MacLean, Houlahan and Barskey, together with Woodsworth's reflections on aging, are the most optimistic answer to this question: they argue for the power of agency and human intention over structural determinants. Let us examine how the relationship between agency and determination might explain the optimism of these writers. A Marxist or neo-Marxist analysis of the relationship between agency and external determinants in the views of older people, whether optimistic or pessimistic, would focus on the connection between *social relations, experiences* and *consciousness*. Briefly, the argument would proceed as follows: the relations of production and social reproduction (the individual history of wage and domestic labour constructed through the social divisions of gender, class and ethnicity) generate a specific set of experiences (of poverty, or financial security or wealth; of dependency or independence) which give rise to particular kinds of consciousness in old age (self-confidence or fear, assertive optimism or depression). One might venture within this analysis to suggest that the optimism of Woodsworth and of the older co-author, Barskey, reflect, above all, their class position and consequent experiences.

But is this determinist perspective, influential in Bicher's essay, the only one we can adopt to account for the different kinds of consciousness in old age? One approach, which we would favour, is to develop a theory of the human subject in old age which is not rigidly determined by previous relationships to structures and ideologies, or through dominant discourses which determine what older people *can* think and feel. This *theory of the subject as agent* stems from Giddens work[1] and is not to be mistaken as a reworking of naive Victorian ideas of "free will" as a way of providing consolation in old age. In this approach, what older people feel, think and do remains determined by their experiences with the economic, social and cultural structures that have impinged upon them throughout their lives—their political participation, their family and religious history, their levels of material existence, the impact of immigration, of cultural minority status, of State health care services, or of the ambiguities involved in receiving support or rejection by caregivers. But this is not a mechanical determinism, because older people reflect intelligently on the events they have lived through, as all of the following essays demonstrate. Also, older people are able to act in a *purposeful* way on the basis of their experiences, within certain constraints and possibilities. These constraints and possibilities (including culturally prescribed repertoires of behaviour, for example, within patriarchal family relations) are provided by the structures that constitute both older people's subjectivity and their environment.

This perspective on the subjectivity of older people suggests that agency and structure are not antagonistic but are closely linked: structures are both determining and enabling. This is, after all, a necessary dialectic; subjects could not exist without the structures that provide possibilities and constraints, and structures could not exist without subjects who reproduce and transform them. A close reading of Woodsworth's essay suggests, indeed, that this perspective on the older person as a human agent within a determining structure is the unstated theoretical underpinning of his account of the "boxes" (gender, class, occupation) which have constrained him throughout his life, but *at the same time* have provided possibilities for breaking out of the constraints and acting more freely upon his intentions. Similar to Bonar's argument that, under certain (cultural) circumstances, older women can increase their status and influence, Woodsworth's view is that, within defined possibilities, agency can actually increase "after retirement." Without doubt this is an encouraging, optimistic view.

What the various studies and reflections contained in this book demonstrate is that the precondition for older people to be able to act as freely and independently as possible, especially in relation to family members, is strongly determined by the availability and control of material resources. If it is true that agency might, for a period, *increase* in old age under optimal conditions, we should investigate as fully as possible, as the various authors of this book do, what those conditions might be. We should not be surprised to find that the first condition is economic.

The Material Experience of Aging Women in Canada

Clearly, the material conditions of older Canadian women are critical in determining the opportunities available to them; and in turn, those opportunities and economic conditions will structure their experience of aging. Under what economic conditions then, will older women live?

At first glance, the extent of poverty among elderly women seems to be relatively moderate, on grounds of both absolute levels and intergenerational equity. For instance, in terms of absolute levels of poverty among the population over fifteen, only 5.7 percent of *wives* over sixty-five in 1987 were found below Statistics Canada poverty lines,[2] although an unsurprising 47 percent of *unattached* women over sixty-five were. Furthermore, the recent historical news sounds positive in terms of its trends: between 1977 and 1987, poverty rates declined for unattached women living outside families, from 77 percent poverty to 47 percent. As for intergenerational equity, more young women, mostly those with dependent children, were poor than were older women. From a male perspective, this evidence appears to indicate general financial well-being for older women with some few regrettable exceptions.

However, when those who qualify for income transfer programmes are analysed, a different picture emerges. Just under half of all seniors qualified for the Guaranteed Income

Supplement, under which all income sources are assessed. This reveals a disturbing correlation between age and poverty, despite recent gains. To whom among the aged population is this direct transfer payment at minimum standard most often directed? For women over sixty-five, the OAS-GIS supplies 43 percent of their income (total average, $11,248) but for men, OAS-GIS is only 25 percent of a much larger income amount (total average, $17,282). At the same time, from occupational pension sources women receive only 31 percent of men's average amounts, and from CPP/QPP less than half of men's average benefits.[3] These figures demonstrate the well-known gender imbalance in incomes for older women.

Most theories on aging reflect a perspective based on male experience and sensibilities. Translated into money outcomes, pension arrangements, both public and private, reflect this viewpoint.[4] In old age, economic vulnerability differs between women and men as it does throughout the rest of their economic lives. One result of this is that for the majority of women, their marital status will determine their material conditions in old age, since poverty is far more pronounced among single elders than among married couples. Given that the gender ratio is unequally distributed across these statuses—most men over sixty-five live with their wives while most women of that age live alone or with relatives—older women are predominantly single and poor. Since the ratio of men to women declines with increasing age, and since men marry younger wives, the older the group, the fewer men. Accordingly, the life patterns of older Canadian men and women differ, and the differences accentuate the older one becomes. Out of one hundred single teenage girls in Canada, eighty-four will find themselves alone some day, a circumstance which is increasing for each age cohort. Not only are poor seniors then, predominantly women, but in absolute dollar amounts the poverty gap by which their incomes fail to meet minimum poverty levels is nearly twice that for single persons as for couples.

That the roles of wife and mother are reified in pension provisions has been pointed out by feminist scholars.[5] Based on the intra-family distribution of income over the life span, negative results of which accumulate with age, women's pension incomes mirror their earlier uncompensated work in old age. The causes are known—the male/female wage gap, women's lower and interrupted labour force participation, women's lower rates of contribution to wage-related pensions (CPP/QPP), women's much lower incidence of private pension-holding and RRSP contributions, their greater share of labour in reproducing and maintaining the labour force, and skewed occupational segregation are consistent historical trends. As well, women now in their sixties, seventies and eighties, came of working age before much social legislation took effect—they were working during the Depression and World War II, and were among those affected by the dominance of the "women-belong-at-home" myth in the 1950s, all specific historical conjunctures which feminist historians show have had strongly negative consequences for women's incomes and ability to save.

Demonstrating these consequences, however, may not by itself evoke policy measures sufficient to change the current proportions of income by gender in old age. In fact, Emily Nett holds that

> demonstrating the source of our dependence and financial condition will *not* elicit the responses we want most from policy makers. Pension reform in favour of women may be an idea that creates far greater fear than correcting our situation.[6]

Why should this be so, that fleshing out the evidence of older women's material poverty should increase rather than decrease public resistance to them? An answer may be suggested by demographic changes in the gender make-up of the elderly.

Why has the prestige of age declined in Canadian society? One suggestion rejects common explanations for devalued status—that the aged lack the vigour required in modern industrial States; that age reminds youth of its mortality; or that generational power struggles are taking place—and points instead to women's growing dominance among the elderly. As much as newly feminized occupations lose prestige when formerly male occupational monopolies shift, so may the increasing identification of women with the aged lead to a decline in the prestige accorded to all elders. Thus, in a society dominated by young and middle-aged men, loss of direct usefulness to that ideologically dominant faction results in a shift toward victim-blaming, with an emphasis on "losses," "our" failure to attract, and finally the "crisis" of the elderly.

Ageism and sexism thus subtly complement one another. One example of the potential for this conjuncture exists in institutionalized settings, occupied largely by older women, where they are particularly vulnerable. Not only are they in danger of being overmedicated with each successive prescription designed to counteract a previous drug's side effects, but their rights and responsibilities may be removed and a process akin to infantilization may operate, where only rarely are their life circumstances addressed by those from whom they seek help.

Indeed, the occurrence of this scenario may increase as the single female aged group grows. In Canada, it has been estimated that the population over sixty-five will double in the next thirty years. Within that older sector itself, the number of those over seventy-five will increase from 40 percent to 70 percent. Finally, prospects for better extended care arrangements will confront the reality that these "older" aged are in direct budgetary competition within provincial budgets with health and postsecondary education in Established Programs Financing.

Thus, both ideological constructs and institutional practice affect elderly women's material conditions. Yet evidence is also available that points toward resistance by elderly women to their assigned devalued status, including older women seeking new positive roles. As the studies by MacLean, Houlahan and Barskey, and Bonar show us, in Canada, the movements for social justice and peace have many elders—especially women—for proponents. One hypothesis for this involvement is that lifelong mistreatment can fuel older women's motivation to seek justice and peace for themselves and others. As well, "postmenopausal zest" appears. In a study of the older cyclist,[7] cross-Canada cyclists were found to have increased self-confidence, endurance, lowered appetite and anxiety, and to have enjoyed the experience. Burwell and Abu-Laban also argue that factors common to many older women's lives (such as later reproductive freedom, greater freedom in sexuality, and increased labour force participation), now lead to a higher status and greater flexibility in their roles. In fact, the evidence is balanced toward rising political awareness for older people, and particularly for older women. What the long-term effects will be on the material conditions of older women is yet to be seen.

What is to be Done?

These essays are not only concerned with the relationship between women, aging and the State, but also with maximizing the space in which older people can act. Within that space, their intentions are to some degree determined by their experiences, including their material conditions, yet our focus is on their potential capacity to engage in collective action. Older people, we wish to emphasize, have great capacity to reflect on what is happening to them; the real question is what can social work and social policy do to aid them in turning their thoughts into action. It is important to stress that they—the social workers and service managers—not appropriate and take over older people (as some have had a tendency to do within feminism, i.e., "explaining" to women what they really want). For example, when David Woodsworth illustrates clearly his experience of deprofessionalization through being seen as an "old man," he is overcoming ageist assumptions that older people are unable to reflect and determine their own priorities. Many younger people, including family members have difficulty acknowledging that older people are capable of being their own agents. Only, however, if older women's basic material conditions are met, will this notion of agency of the self be more than a convenient ignoring of need. Evidence is found throughout this book (especially in the essays by Aronson, Bicher, Bonar) that those who succeed the most in maintaining autonomy and interdependence are those who do not have to worry deeply about money, and that when poverty forces them into one-sided exchange relationships they have no agency, hence no autonomy or true interconnectedness.

Notes

1. See: Giddens 1981 and Sewell 1990.
2. Statistics Canada has thirty-three levels of poverty based on family size, city size, and region of the country. Recent work on poverty has also focused on the depth of poverty, or the distribution of a given population below the poverty line; i.e. the poorest poor.
3. National Council of Welfare 1992.
4. Havens 1983; Dulude 1981.
5. Lizee 1981; Dulude 1981.
6. Nett 1982, p. 229.
7. Mittleman, et al., 1989.

References

Abu-Laban, Sharon McIrvin (1984). "Health and the older woman," *Canadian Woman Studies,* 1 & 4: 19-25.

Burwell, Elinor J. (1984). "Sexism in social science research on aging," in *Taking Sex into Account: The Policy Consequences of Sexist Research,* by Jill McCalla Vickers, ed., Ottawa: Carleton University Press.

Dulude, Louise (1981). *Pension Reform with Women in Mind.* Ottawa: Canadian Advisory Council on the Status of Women.

Fletcher, Susan and Stone, Leroy O. (1982). *The Living Arrangements of Canada's Older Women.* Ottawa: Statistics Canada, Cat. 86-503, Ministry of Supply and Services.

Gee, Ellen Margaret and Kimball, Meredith M. (1987). *Women and Aging.* Toronto: Butterworths.

Giddens, Anthony (1981). *A Contemporary Critique of Historical Materialism.* London: Macmillan.

Gold, Dolores (1984). "Sex differences in the experience of aging," *Canadian Woman Studies,* 5-3: 32-34.

Havens, Betty and Chappell, Neena L. (1983). "Triple jeopardy: Age, sex and ethnicity," *Canadian Ethnic Studies,* 15-3: 119-132.

Lizee, Ruth Rose (1981). *La réforme des pensions: Quels sont les enjeux pour les femmes?* Montréal: Université du Québec à Montréal.

McDaniel, Susan A. (1988). "Older women: Their quest for justice and peace," *Canadian Woman Studies,* 9-1: 78-80.

Mittleman, Karen; Crawford, Susan; Holliday, Stephen; Gutman, Gloria; and Bhakthan, Gordon (1989). "The older cyclist: Anthropometric, physiological, and psychosocial changes observed during a Trans-Canada cycle tour," *Canadian Journal on Aging,* 8-1: 144-156.

National Council of Welfare (1992). *Poverty Profile, 1980-1990.* Ottawa: Ministry of Supply and Services.

Nett, Emily M. (1982). *Family Studies of Elders: Gerontological and Feminist Approaches.* Ottawa: Canadian Sociology and Anthropology Association.

Neysmith, Sheila M. (1982). "Aging in Canada: The making of a social problem," *Social Development Issues,* 6-1: 27-40.

Sewell, William J., Jr. (1990). "How classes are made: Critical reflections on E.P. Thompson's theory of working class formation," in H.J. Kaye and K. McClelland (eds.), *E.P. Thompson: Critical Perspectives.* Temple.

1

Old Women and Care: Choice or Compulsion?

Jane Aronson

The perspectives of old people are seldom considered central to the debates about health and social care in an aging society. We hear more commonly of alarm at rising government expenditure on social programmes and of the health care system straining to accommodate increasing numbers of elderly patients. Governmental interest in containing the potential demand for health and social services tends to be accompanied by affirmation of "the family" as the proper and most effective locus of assistance to old people. Reflecting the degree to which government services are kept in the background, it is estimated that only 10-15 percent of the total care of old people originates in the public sector; the balance, 85-90 percent, is provided informally, generally by female relatives. Some aspects of this pattern of obligation and responsibility and of its impact on caregivers have received attention over the last ten or fifteen years. However, the perspectives of old people in need of care—who, like their caregivers, are mainly women—have received relatively little exposure. Lack of attention given to their experience relegates them to a passive role—the objects rather than the subjects of care.

The purpose of this essay is to contribute to the emerging literature on older women requiring care, thereby bringing them from the margin to the centre of the debate about the care of the aged. The character of the prevailing debate and the depiction of old people will be briefly outlined. This will set the social context for considering the information drawn from a recent study of women as givers and receivers of care in middle and later life.[1] This information will then provide the basis for discussion of alternative ways of meeting older women's needs for assistance, and of the importance of creating the conditions in which they can assert their own definitions of their problems and exert some control over the resolution of these problems.

Care of Old People: The Shape of Current Debate

A review of government statements concerning old people suggests that the central concerns for public policy lie in containing government expenditure and sustaining patterns of informal care. Preoccupation with limiting spending is exemplified in a recent federal government working paper:

> There are some obvious economies if older people are able to continue living in the community. They exercise varying degrees of self-care; they may have family members, neighbours

and friends who can perform essential tasks for them; they may receive various types of voluntary services and help.[2]

This emphasis on shifting responsibility to the informal sphere rests on assumptions about the place of families in supporting elderly kin. While reference is often made to a range of informal resources (neighbours, friends, volunteers), the reality that female family members provide the most enduring and substantial support has been consistently documented.[3] Recognition of this reality emerges in policy makers' concerns that, with women's increasing participation in the paid labour force, the critical pool of unpaid female family caregivers may diminish.

Governmental interest in sustaining—not changing—the balance of responsibility between formal and informal spheres is expressed specifically in guidelines for service and programme planning. For example, one of the objectives of the "one-stop shopping" strategy proposed in Ontario is:

to avoid excessive professionalization and to enhance and supplement, not replace, existing or potential family and volunteer support services.[4]

Old people's interests in the structure of such care arrangements receive little or no direct mention. The assumption that their families are the most appropriate locus for their care is left unstated and questions of appropriateness *for whom* are not raised.

Depictions of old people and the health care system in the media and popular discussion mirror policy makers' and politicians' concerns with government expenditure, often in tones of alarm and apprehension about the growing "burden" of the elderly population. For example, in an article entitled "Bed Blockers Blamed for Emergency Ward Crunch," D. Grant quotes the executive director of the Hospital Council of Metro Toronto.[5] He describes long-term care patients as: "imposing on the system. Nobody wants them. The hospitals don't. The families don't and certainly the government doesn't."

The devaluing and blaming language in this portrayal of old people is a theme identified and analyzed more fully in the U.S. and the U.K., where cuts and restraint in government spending on social programmes and an associated belt-tightening rhetoric are more advanced.[6] Old people are regarded as motivated actors, burdening over-taxed societies with their needs. Extreme solutions to the problems they present therefore seem warranted, expectations are lowered and sacrifices justified to avert fiscal crisis. While we do not yet hear official language of such a victim-blaming nature in Canada, it is only a small step away from the commonly-heard attribution of an incipient health care funding crisis to population aging.

A review of research and writing in social gerontology suggests that academic activity has mirrored the prevailing focus of the debate presented above. There has also been a central focus on sustaining the broad pattern of care and division of responsibilities between the State and families.

The ubiquitousness of studies of caregiver stress and coping, especially in North American gerontology, implicitly feeds policy objectives to keep responsibility for care out of the formal sector by deflecting it, with minimal investment, back to the private sphere. Often, without making its assumptions explicit, research on caregiver stress and burden is cast in relation to containing the potential demand for public services and bolstering conventional notions of family obligations and women's adjustment to their domestic roles.[7]

Analyses of social policy and gender relations have introduced a critical strand into the literature on informal care. Instead of taking women's unpaid work for granted as essential labour in the social arrangements for the care of old people (and other groups deemed dependent), women as caregivers have come into focus in terms of their own welfare and needs.[8] This critique has clarified the impact of social policies and institutional practices on shaping and enforcing the division of formal and informal spheres. It has also generated a wealth of questions about the division of responsibility for caring work between men and women and between individuals and government.

* * *

Analysis and questioning of the experiences of old people in need of care is much less well-developed. Old women's views are seldom represented in studies on caregiving and support in the informal sector. Nor, until recently, have they been included in analyses of the welfare State and women. The concerns of younger women have tended to dominate.

Old Women's Experiences of Needing Care

Over the last ten years, we have seen growing interest in issues concerning older women and, as a result, there is now available a basic descriptive picture of women in later life that covers such dimensions as income and poverty, work and retirement, widowhood, social and family life, and health. Feminist perspectives on these studies draw connections between the structured economic disadvantage of old women, its roots in lifelong economic dependency and social subordination, and a general social context characterized by ageism and sexism that grant old women a precarious social status.

However, there has been relatively little attention paid to old women's experiences of being cared for by family members. Evers' valuable work in examining how elderly women respond to receiving care suggests the complexity of desired or tolerable levels of independence and dependence, and underscores the need to recognize individuality in a population that is, all too often, treated as a homogeneous category. In her study of mothers receiving care from daughters, she found simultaneous experiences of warmth, satisfaction, conflict and ambivalence.[9]

In the absence of more direct study of the subjective experience of needing the care of younger female relatives, research on elderly people receiving formal care in institutional contexts provides some useful insights. The greater likelihood of female rather than male patients being labelled as problematic has been observed in several studies.[10] Exploring the process of requiring care suggests particular complexities for women in relinquishing their lifelong identities as carers and nurturers and handing over responsibility for self-care to other, younger women. Autobiographical and fictional accounts of this transition yield particularly rich and revealing images of women's efforts to fend off diminishment and vulnerability[11] and we are beginning to see older women writing to stir collective consciousness and voice anger at the diminishment and marginalization they experience.[12]

The Study

This study sought to contribute to the exploration of older women's subjective experiences. In order to find women who had experienced needing care, I approached an Ontario association of retired women teachers. Members in the Toronto area responded to a newsletter announcement concerning the research, identifying themselves as aging women who had adult daughters and who experienced concerns about their present or future need for assistance. Initial respondents introduced me to interested colleagues and peers in a snowball fashion. Thus, I located fourteen women between the ages of fifty-nine and eighty-five; all were white and none described experiencing serious financial hardship.

Building on observations of the early stages of social movements and challenges to the status quo, I sought a middle-class sample of this kind with the expectation that—

having worked in the paid labour force and accustomed to some degree of independence—they would be more likely to identify tensions in their capacities and situations in later life. In the interests of maximizing and exploring this aspect of women's experiences, I did not introduce variation in social class and ethnicity. This sampling decision points clearly to important ways of expanding the focus of the data presented below. Specifically, comparative study of other groups of women (e.g., working-class women, women without children, women of different racial backgrounds and immigration experiences) would yield interesting theoretical insights.

Through interviews I explored with the women how they saw or anticipated their needs for support; their thoughts and feelings about themselves; their recollections about their own mothers who had lived to grow old; the degree to which others—either friends, family or formal service providers— were involved in their situations; their general ideas about family ties and the place of public or formal service provision for the elderly; and key aspects of their biographies, work lives and family histories.

The interview material constituted both individual descriptions of fourteen women's realities and "points of entry" into the wider social and economic processes that frame them.[13] In reviewing the transcripts, I identified themes in the women's accounts and explored the connections between them to build up an overarching pattern of analysis that could be linked to relevant conceptual frameworks.[14] Two critical aspects of the analysis are presented below.

The Contradictory Experience of Needing Support

Speaking in general terms about the process of growing older and the context of family ties, the older women who took part in the study confirmed prevailing assumptions about family obligations. That adult children would step in to assist elderly parents was seen as a "natural" process, motivated variously by affection, reciprocity and a sense of duty. Many respondents could recall this process in relation to their own mothers in the past. Reflecting prevailing norms concerning gender roles and the normative patterning of responsibility in families, respondents also noted their "good fortune" at having daughters and their sympathy for age peers who did not or, even worse, who had no children at all.

While recognizing and valuing these cultural assumptions about family ties, respondents experienced difficulty in translating them into the realities of their lives. The process of translation was complicated by their adherence to other strongly-held cultural images concerning appropriate conduct in later life. For example, women expressed the wish to not be a "burden" to their children. This sentiment, frequently heard among old people, compelled them not to "impose" and to "let children live their own lives." They also upheld notions of independence and self-sufficiency and distanced themselves from older mothers who were "needy," "demanding" or "dependent," stressing the importance of being free-standing and self-reliant.

However, this adherence to cultural values of independence and self-reliance ran counter to the reality of facing the prospect of relying on others for assistance. Thus, they confronted the dilemma of trying to balance real insecurities and needs for assistance with cultural demands to be independent by setting limits on their conduct and feelings, so that the underlying dilemma was contained, evaded or managed in some fashion.

For example, they set limits in the form of assertions about never sharing a household with a daughter, maintaining clear financial boundaries and ensuring that their exchanges were as reciprocal as possible. More than simply a casual preference, limit-setting suggested resistance and self-preservation in relation to forces perceived to be threatening or intrusive in some way and represented respondents' efforts to impose some degree of control on the tensions they experienced in needing support. Regardless of the particularities, respondents' limit-setting centred on the ways in which they would ask for or be prepared to accept help. An eighty-two year old respondent articulated the conditions under which she accepted her daughter's or son-in-law's help in order to minimize her sense of diminishment:

> So they say: "Well, you know, just give us your laundry every week." And they do it. And they take me shopping nearly every week ... in ways like that they really help, you know. And they don't make a big song and a dance about it and I don't. I'm grateful and I let them know, but, you know, it's not "poor granny" or any of that at all.

Many respondents couched their limits in terms of their daughters' interests rather than their own. They sought to protect their daughters from over-extending themselves and thus, perhaps, derived some satisfaction from their continued position in mothering and caretaking:

> I do know that I will try that route (a home for the aged) rather than going to live with my daughter. I don't want to do that, I don't want to put any extra burdens on her.

In order to uphold successfully individualistic values of independence and maintain a sense of integrity, respondents effectively suppressed their own needs and wishes. The account of a seventy-four year old women illustrates this process. She had raised her only daughter alone, after leaving her husband soon after they were married. She had led a particularly independent life, supporting herself as a teacher throughout. After enjoying the early years of her retirement, she had experienced serious health problems and spoke anxiously of the future, worrying that she might not be able to stay alone in her apartment. She reflected on her contact with her daughter and son-in-law:

> Once in a while, I get kind of depressed, low-spirited and I miss them, not seeing them. I think: "Oh, grow up will you! You know, they can't be running over here at night to see me after their work." But I feel that they're doing all they *can* do. And I don't want to be one of these possessive

mothers that just ... will act the martyr or ... play
dependent, you know, at all. I like to be able to live
my own life and see them in a nice social way.

I asked her if she ever shared her low-spirited mood with her
daughter. She replied with a nervous laugh: "I wouldn't dare
show it to her. I'd be ashamed, kind of ashamed."

Drawing on a sociological analysis of feelings, Shott
describes shame, like guilt, as a reflexive role-taking emotion
that is "... provoked by the realization that others (or the
generalized other) consider one's *self* deficient."[15] Thus, to
preserve a socially acceptable sense of self and protect herself
from shame, this respondent contains her low spirits, masks
her anxieties and bolsters her self-esteem by distancing herself from women who do not live up to this standard of behaviour. She is a harsh critic of her own experience, her
incorporated beliefs permitting no compassion for her own
difficulties and tensions.

Another respondent, in quite poor health, seemed to have
the emotional detachment to articulate this privately experienced dilemma as she anticipated a discrepancy between
the socially appropriate behaviour for an aging mother and
her own needs and capacities:

I suppose I don't want to be any sort of burden to
her, in any way. That includes an emotional drain
on her time, as well as the physical. Now, am I
just saying that—just paying lip service to it?
This is what I know I *should* say and I *should* say

and I *should* feel. Do I *really* feel that way? I don't know. Perhaps … when the time comes, I'll be a real clinging vine. You know, it appals me, the thought—but, however, maybe I would be—I'd certainly try not to be.

Preserving pride emerged as the opposite of failing to behave appropriately and fending off shame. A sixty-six year old respondent remembered her own, now dead, mother's inability to tell her what she needed and what concerned her as she aged. She recalled how much this inability irritated her. She had wished that her mother would simply express her needs straight-forwardly rather than, as she felt, avoid the subject. Now a widow and in poor health herself, her mother's reserve had come to make sense to her. She understood that her mother was "protecting her pride" and finds herself doing the same thing, setting limits on the degree to which she reveals her anxieties to her children or asks them for support. Pride derives from knowing one has behaved in accordance with normative expectations and, like shame, signals the degree to which cultural prescriptions and socially approved ideas about receiving help and old age are embedded in individuals' inner experiences. Effectively, these internalized forces operate as an invisible form of social control.

Experience of a Marginal and Precarious Social Status

Tensions in subjects' experiences were exacerbated by their marginal and precarious social status. Describing their social contexts in very broad terms, respondents often experienced their age as a negative characteristic and reported feeling disadvantaged in such public settings as the workplace and in such routine processes as shopping and securing goods and services. More critically, in the context of this essay, they also felt themselves to be marginal in relation to the health and social services and their own families.

While respondents reported some positive encounters with the health and social service system, their impressions generally left them apprehensive and pessimistic. The lack of interest of family doctors was explained in a matter-of-fact way as the result of the low priority and urgency given to old people's complaints. Respondents' observations of peers' or relatives' experiences in institutional settings confirmed their concerns about the quality of care:

> I haven't *any* thought of retirement homes. I hear people talk of them. Mother was in a nursing home and that was enough to put me off for the rest of my life. And, oh, it was one of those glossy places with the great big rotundas and whatnot and when you got up above the first floor, you really knew what was going on ... it was dreadful ... people aren't even treated like human beings.

Underlying their distaste at the prospect of being "herded together" and patronized was a dread of "being ruled" and losing control of their lives.

Related to these apprehensions about the nature of formally provided services, respondents also felt they were not entitled to them. One woman stopped abruptly while reflecting on the ways of designing institutions to give residents more private space by saying: "But it'd cost the kind of money they don't have, you see." Others noted that "we can't expect much" and "felt sorry for the younger generation because there are so many of us to support now." Such comments suggest that the burdensome portrayals of the elderly discussed above are accepted as facts and inevitabilities.[16] They are, thus, effective in justifying the limits of public services and discounting complaints or visions of other possibilities.

Respondents' sense of disentitlement in the context of government services was parallelled in their recognition of their marginal status in the context of their families. The strongly-held wish not to "burden" or "impose" on their children suggests a precarious status and the need for care and watchfulness in making demands. For example, in the words of two women:

> They're very nice and very supportive to a point. But they have their own families and their association with me—naturally, they're fond of me and they'd be upset if anything happened to me—but they can live, each one of them, as a family group ... without me.

> I think it's very important to people to have their own life and their own lifestyle, because

children, no matter how good they are, don't appreciate having somebody to be saddled with.

These observations illustrate the primacy accorded to the nuclear family; the claims of spouses and children were understood to come before those of elderly parents. Some respondents identified this taken-for-granted ordering of priorities across two generations—their own earlier views of their elderly mothers echoing in the tenuous claims they now felt they had upon their adult children:

> As my son said to me at one point: "Mum, I'll come and help you as much as I can, but my first obligation's to my own family—you know, to my wife and children." And I thought that was kind of callous ... and then I thought afterwards: "I did the *same* thing, you know, with my mother."

Such taken-for-granted recognition of old women's marginal social status, together with the tensions embedded in respondents' experiences of needing support, resulted in a perplexing awareness of jeopardy and absence of choice. For example, a seventy-nine year old woman suffering from increasingly debilitating arthritis expressed approval of the general notion of children's obligation to parents, and recalled how she had gone to considerable lengths to look after her own mother, a generation before. For her husband's "toleration" of her daily visits to her mother, she was grateful and appreciative, feeling that he had "put up with more than most men would":

> I think they (children) should be sympathetic ... but I certainly don't think they should give up their youth and be *dominated* by a parent ... I certainly don't. That becomes a worry when you're over seventy. If anything should happen ... I almost made my daughter promise, I said: "Please don't put me in a home" ... I'm in that position where I just worry about the end of life. Who *is* going to ...?

This respondent illustrates the disjunctures rooted in elderly women's experiences. She feels the inconsistencies between her qualified belief in children's obligation, her memories of the personal costs of caring for her own mother, her lack of confidence and anxiety as she becomes increasingly frail, her apprehension at the prospect of institutional care and, ultimately, her reluctant dependence on her daughter to protect her from such a fate. This dependence would evidently be unwelcome to her even as it is made necessary by public policies that don't provide acceptable alternatives.

Discussion

The exploratory nature of the research reported in this paper and the narrowness of the white, middle-class sample clearly cannot generate definitive conclusions. However, the research points to the complexity of older women's experiences and offers insight into the broad social and ideological forces that frame them.

The contradictions that emerged in respondents' accounts—between needing assistance, wanting security, not wanting to impose on others, upholding values of self-reliance and independence, feeling precarious and socially marginal, and wanting to hide feelings of weakness or anxiety—were deeply embedded in their senses of themselves. This embedding of public ideology and personal experience corresponds to theoretical perspectives that stress the unity of individual experience and wider social processes and the complex reproduction of social structure in everyday life.[17]

Specifically, structuring the experiences of the respondents were cultural prescriptions concerning family ties, the proper conduct of old women and the high value attached to individualism—images reinforced by social policies. Influenced by their particular biographies and resources, respondents were tenacious in trying to exert some influence over their circumstances in this complex ideological context, although, as we have seen, their efforts—in the form of limit-setting and containing feelings—often led to the stifling of their needs and the confirmation of their marginal status. This tension and complexity contradicts the assumptions of social policies discussed earlier, that construe old people as passive participants in an unproblematic process of receiving assistance.

The women who took part in this study placed their experiences of old age in the context of their lifetimes—lifetimes in which many had, typically, found themselves in supportive

positions in relation to their own mothers. The fallacy of identifying women as either givers or takers, fixing them in static
generational positions with conflicting interests is thus
clarified. Instead, we see that the continuity of cultural expectations of women over the life course—in giving primacy to
others and subordinating their own needs—unites their experiences.

Difficult individual experiences of having an "uncaring"
daughter or an "ungrateful," "manipulative" or "burdensome" mother certainly exist and are suggestive of intergenerational opposition rather than this commonality in
experience. However, interpersonal tensions are under-
standable as just one aspect of a total picture of care in which,
on the one hand, female kin are generally made responsible
for solutions to older people's needs and, on the other, older
women are discouraged from feeling confident about expressing their needs and making claims for assistance. The
relationships between women of different generations are,
thus, heavily loaded with expectations and constraints which
are sometimes, unsurprisingly, manifest in the form of interpersonal strain. The limited availability of publicly provided
services and supports is a significant ingredient in producing
such strain. If services were more generously and readily
available, women of all ages would have greater opportunity
to structure their own exchanges and relationships and to
determine their own pathways through middle and later life.
It is crucial, then, to recognize that women's experiences
occur in a coercive context in that provision and receipt of
care between women in families is made necessary by public

policies and cultural forces that inhibit the development of alternatives. Thus, the real opposition of interests exists, not between women giving and receiving care, but between women and the State. Identification of division between generations of women is a diversion from this more fundamental conflict and from consideration of alternative social arrangements for responding to old people's needs.

As noted earlier, the tendency to separate caregivers' and receivers' interests has been reflected in the emphases of research and writing in gerontology, feminist social science and analyses of social policy. Thus, we know more of the "compulsory altruism"[18] expected of care providers than we do of what may be called—based on the empirical data presented here—the "compulsory acquiescence" expected of care-receivers. Continued efforts to remedy this imbalance are important for the future.

Expecting that increased research attention to elderly women will influence public policy in a direct or immediate way is unrealistic. However, making their experiences of needing assistance more visible in the debate may validate and highlight the significance of their concerns. The positive impact that previous studies on the nature of social problems and social movements have had on other marginalized groups, suggests the possibilities for gradual social change and a shift in consciousness.[19] For example, studies of housewives in the 1960s and 1970s directed attention to work and experience that were previously unacknowledged.[20] That housework was written about at all lent it some legitimacy and, in addition, the research produced images of women's experiences that they could then recognize, challenge or dismiss, give words to and discuss.

Debate about housework and child care spread, over a period of time, from the domain of "experts" to become the stuff of more everyday conversation. While there have been only relatively small changes in the organization of unpaid domestic work and in the distribution of responsibility for child care, the issues posed for women are now speakable and very much in the public arena.

Similarly, writing about elderly women's experiences as recipients of care may contribute to making previously hidden issues and concerns thinkable and speakable, as well as more central to the debate about care provision. The long-term goal is to provide the kinds of supportive environments and assistance that they would like to see, and to foster the conditions in which elderly women are able to express their needs, since their current actions and perspectives cannot be understood as necessarily reflecting real preferences. Mindful of the oppressive ideological and social constraints experienced by the women in the study reported here, it would be erroneous to regard their wish to strive relentlessly for self-sufficiency, without fully expressing their needs, as an exercise of choice. To return to the experience of the woman quoted above who expected little of public services and felt apprehensive about the care that was provided, for her, the prospect of dependence on her daughter was preferable to institutionalization. However, her reluctant position can hardly be seen as a choice; rather, it represents an instance of the "compulsory acquiesence" identified earlier. In fact, we know very little about how elderly women would like to achieve security and assistance if they did have real choices among a range of truly acceptable alternatives.

The alternatives identified in current discussions of social responses to the elderly tend to revolve around the conceptual categories of informal care, home or community care and institutional care. Such research is, understandably, obscured in the immediate and pragmatic concerns regarding the relative costs and interrelationships of the three approaches, although we are beginning to see more open-minded considerations of future possibilities.

In such discussions, community care, rather than congregate care, is generally favoured. It is seen to be responsive to old people's generally understood wishes to stay in their own homes and sustain as much independence and privacy as possible. Visions of good community care include notions of a real partnership between women and the State, respect for the individuality of family care relationships, while bearing in mind the potential for exploitation of women's paid and unpaid labour.[21]

In an attempt to envision some essential ingredients of good residential care, Dalley begins by noting that, as a fundamental condition, dependent people must be assured of basic economic security. Her envisioned principles for collective living stress that people must be able to control their life choices, that systems of care provision must be responsive to individuals' changing wishes and abilities, and that responsibility for care must be shared in a way that ensures stability and continuity for the care recipient. Such visionary thinking about the possibilities of congregate care is hampered by the weight of the long accumulation of research on the negative aspects of institutions and by old people's often quoted aversion to the available institutional options.

By recognizing the mistake in understanding old people's current conduct and opinions as reflecting genuine choices, we can see how over-hasty dismissal of residential forms of care would be unfortunate. Dalley underscores the danger of allowing the current patterning of care to limit our visions for the future. She points to collective living and support arrangements that are, or have been, in some cases, well-regarded. Thus, she emphasizes the degree to which our visions are social constructions rather than essential realities. Accordingly, the nature of institutions and the meanings of dependence can change since they are culturally and historically specific concepts.

The study of cases where elderly women have had the resources and capacities to shape the conditions under which they obtain support in old age may be revealing in this regard. Dalley suggests, for example, that retirement villages and life-care communities in the U.S. may represent examples of chosen collective living. So, too, may discussions among members of the Toronto-based Older Women's Network about the possibility of establishing a housing co-operative, and instances such as the house shared by five elderly women friends with a hired housekeeper described by one of the study respondents. Such situations—currently the experiences of relatively few and, often, relatively materially privileged older women—can liberate our visions of what is possible and inform and modify our conceptions of care provision. Exploration of circumstances where groups of women—large or small, formal or informal—try to work toward determining the conditions of their old age can also shed light on the structural barriers to such collective activity.[22]

In a collection of essays about her own aging, Barbara MacDonald reflects on ageism as a critical barrier to the development among old women of a strong collective identity and as a source of division between women of different ages. She describes, with disappointment and anger, her experience in the women's movement of feeling invisible and "other"— by virtue of being old. In an essay entitled "An Open Letter to the Women's Movement," she makes some suggestions to younger women for working on the ageism that is so deeply embedded in contemporary culture. Her words illuminate vividly the main themes of this essay:

> Don't feel guilty. You will then avoid us because you are afraid we might become dependent and you know you can't meet our needs. Don't burden us with *your* idea of dependency and *your* idea of obligation.[23]

> Don't think that an old woman has always been old. She is in the process of discovering what seventy, eighty and ninety mean. As more and more old women talk and write about the reality of this process, in a world that negates us, we will all discover how revolutionary that is.[24]

Notes

1. Aronson 1988.
2. Health and Welfare Canada, 1986, p. 4.
3. Bulmer 1987.
4. Ontario Office for Senior citizens' Affairs, 1987, p. 10.
5. Grant 1985.
6. Minkler 1983.
7. Moroney 1980.
8. Finch and Groves 1983.
9. Evers 1985.
10. Rosenthal et al., 1980.
11. Laurence 1964; Lessing 1984.
12. MacDonald 1984; Marshall 1987.
13. Smith 1986, p. 7.
14. Bulmer 1979.
15. Shott 1979, p. 1325.
16. Minkler 1983.
17. Leonard 1984; Smith 1986.
18. Land and Rose 1985.
19. Margolis 1985; Spector and Kitsuse 1977.
20. Oakley 1974.
21. Finch 1984; Ungerson 1987.
22. Ralph 1988.
23. MacDonald 1984, p. 74.
24. Ibid., pp. 74-75.

References

Aronson, J. (1988). "Women's Experiences in Giving and Receiving Care: Pathways to Social Change." Ph.D. Dissertation, University of Toronto.

Bulmer, M. (1979). "Concepts in the Analysis of Qualitative Data." *Sociological Review,* 27(4): 651-677.

Bulmer, M. (1987). *The Social Basis of Community Care.* London: Allen and Unwin.

Dalley, G. (1988). *Ideologies of Caring: Rethinking Community and Collectivism.* London: Macmillan.

Evers, H. (1981). "Care or Custody? The Experiences of Women Patients in Long-Stay Geriatric Wards." In B. Hutter and G. Williams (eds.), *Con-*

trolling Women: The Normal and the Deviant. London: Croom Helm (pp. 108-130).

Evers, H. (1985). "The Frail Elderly Woman: Emergent Questions in Aging and Woman's Health." In E. Lewin and V. Oleson (eds.), *Women, Health and Illness.* New York: Tavistock (pp. 86-112).

Finch, J. (1984). "Community Care: Developing Non-Sexist Alternatives." *Critical Social Policy,* 9: 6-18.

Finch, J. and Groves, D. (eds.). (1983). *A Labour of Love: Women, Work and Caring.* London: Routledge and Kegan Paul.

Grant, D. (1985). "'Bed-Blockers,' Blamed for Emergency Ward Crunch." *The Globe and Mail,* February 18, p. 16.

Health and Welfare Canada. (1986). *Aging: Shifting the Emphasis.* Working Paper.

Land, H. and Rose, H. (1985). "Compulsory Altruism for Some or an Altruistic Society for All?" In P. Bean, J. Ferris and D. Whynes (eds.), *In Defence of Welfare.* London: Tavistock (pp. 74-96).

Laurence, M. (1964). *The Stone Angel.* Toronto: McClelland and Stewart.

Leonard, P. (1984). *Personality and Ideology: Towards a Materialist Understanding of the Individual.* London: Macmillan.

Lessing, D. (1984). *The Diaries of Jane Somers.* London: Michael Joseph.

MacDonald, B. with Rich, C. (1984). *Look Me in the Eye: Old Women, Aging and Ageism.* San Francisco: Spinsters Ink.

Margolis, D.R. (1985). "Redefining the Situation: Negotiations on the Meaning of 'Woman.'" *Social Problems,* 32(4): 332-347.

Marshall, D. (1987). *Silver Threads: Critical Reflections on Growing Old.* Toronto: Between the Lines.

Minkler, M. (1983). "Blaming the Aged Victim: The Politics of Scapegoating in Times of Fiscal Conservatism." *International Journal of Health Services,* 13(1): 155-167.

Moroney, R. (1980). *Families, Social Services and Social Policy: The Issue of Shared Responsibility.* Rockville, MD: National Institute of Mental Health.

Oakley, A. (1974). *Housewife.* London: Allen Lane.

Ontario Office for Senior Citizens' Affairs. (1987). *"One Stop Shopping": An Integrated Approach to Community Health and Social Services.* Consultation Tour.

Ralph, D. (1988). "Researching from the Bottom: Lessons Participatory Research has for Feminists." *Canadian Review of Social Policy,* 22:36-40.

Rosenthal, C.J., Marshall, V.W., MacPherson, A.S., and French, S.E. (1980). *Nurses, Patients and Families.* London: Croom Helm.

Shott, S. (1979). "Emotion and Social Life: A Symbolic Interaction Analysis." *American Journal of Sociology,* 84:1317-1334.

Smith, D.E. (1986). "Institutional Ethnography: A Feminist Method. *Resources for Feminist Research,*" 15(1): 6-13.

Spector, M. and Kitsuse, J. (1977). *Constructing Social Problems.* Menlo Park, CA: Cummings Publishing Company.

Ungerson, C. (1987). *Policy is Personal: Sex, Gender and Informal Care.* London: Tavistock.

2

The Dependency Relationship Between Daughters and Mothers

Marilyn Bicher

Introduction

Over the last ten years, my interest in the life and times of elderly people has increased. I have watched elderly relatives and clients become physically and emotionally dependent, socially isolated, and economically vulnerable. Often elderly people become unnecessarily dependent because of social barriers to their independence: the division of labour within the family, inadequate retirement wages, poor transportation systems, the high cost of housing, and inadequate community support. These factors contribute to the general dependence of elderly people, and in particular to the dependency relationship between elderly mothers and their daughters.

The term dependency is often used in existing literature on the elderly as one that encompasses emotional, social, economic and physical aspects of dependence. However, some work has been done that offers a more in-depth critique of the notion of dependency. Walker, for example, distinguishes among the four forms of dependency mentioned above and explains how social policy exacerbates the dependence of vulnerable elderly people. Eichenbaum and Orbach and Rubin discuss emotional dependency and claim that, within limitations, it is a healthy human need, but question the social arrangements surrounding emotional dependency. In fact, each type of dependency ought to be analyzed both individually and in relation to one another. By doing this, one may begin to understand how each form is created and reinforced in our society.

* * *

Elderly people in Canada experience many barriers to independent living.[1] These barriers and the limited support provided to older people encourage dependence on family members and/or the State. Based on the 1981 Canadian census, 38 percent of non-institutionalized elderly people in Québec lived in multigenerational households.[2] In the United States, approximately five million people are providing care to a parent at any one moment.[3] In Canada, only 2 percent of people between sixty-five and sixty-nine, and 37 percent of people (mostly women) over eighty-five were living in institutions in 1986.[4] These statistics indicate that most elderly women and men live either on their own or with a family member. Even among the elderly people living on their own or in institutions, some of them are likely to receive emotional and/or economic and/or physical support from family members. In most cases, it is the daughters and daughters-in-law who are the primary caregivers.[5] My own experience working with elderly people supports these findings. Moreover, I noticed that when respite care was offered to some daughters, resistance to accepting this support came both from the mothers and the daughters. This indicates to me that psychic structures are not separate from social structures but "reveal the working of society in each individual,"[6] as daughter and mother both felt it was the daughter's job to provide care.

In this essay, the structural and psychological dimensions of the older mother and middle-aged daughter relationship will be discussed. In order to suggest interventions that would aptly support this population, an understanding of the dynamics of this particular relationship is necessary. One would have to ask what are the social structures affecting the psychic structures of women? How do the barriers to independence maintain social structures and create and reinforce dependency between an older mother and her middle-aged daughter?

To discover some answers to these questions, two main bodies of feminist literature were reviewed. The first is composed of feminist adaptations of object relations theory, a psychological theory that explains the dependency relationship between mother and daughter. It looks at the initial bonding relationship as well as the role and position of women in a patriarchal culture. The second is the social construction perspective. This perspective explains the mother/daughter dependency relationship by looking at social structures and analyzing the material conditions of women and elderly people. Each perspective contributes valuable insight but fails to provide an adequate link to the other. Since psychic structures are not separate from social structures, the psychological and sociological perspectives ought to be viewed separately, and then as they interrelate.

To test some of the assumptions in these theoretical approaches, eleven in-depth interviews with five mothers and each of their daughters were carried out. The five mothers ranged in age from seventy-two to eighty-four while the six daughters ranged in age from thirty-seven to fifty. In this sample, one mother was married and all others were widowed. All five women had some income in addition to pension. One woman did qualify for the Guaranteed Income Supplement; however, she was living rent free in a house owned by her son. Economic dependency was not a real issue for any of these women and only one mother was physically dependent. While each felt that they could perform less than in the past, all assessed their health as good. Two of the mothers lived in their own apartments, two lived in a house, and the mother who was most dependent was living in a seniors' residence. Of the daughters, one was single and was living alone, while all the others were married and had children living at home. All were in the paid labour force.

The goal of the study was, firstly, to find out if mothers and daughters could identify forces that encouraged dependence, and secondly, if mothers are dependent on daughters and/or vice versa, how are they dependent, how do they feel about it, and what are their expectations and recommendations for change? The findings were used to discuss implications for social policy and social work practice.

Object Relations Theory

There are two underlying assumptions in object relations theory as feminist scholars have adapted it. First, it is believed that the nature of the relationship between mother and child is determined by the fact that the mother is a woman in a patriarchal society. Second, the mother's unconscious feelings about the sex of her infant will affect the mother and child relationship.[7]

In Chodorow's examination of the internalized oppression of the mother/daughter relationship, she focuses on the earliest phases of life. Here, the infant, male or female, is born with self-centredness. The world revolves around her and her primary caregiver, which in our society is the woman—mother. The primary caregiver is perceived by the infant to be an extension of itself. Differentiation occurs when the infant begins to see "the self" as distinct from the other—the object (caregiver-mother). Chodorow's main thesis is that girls grow up with a sense of continuity and oneness with their mothers, and thus have trouble with differentiation and separation.[8] If this is so, then one might deduce that the dependency relationship between middle-aged daughters and elderly mothers is a continuation of this phenomenon.

On the other hand, male children have less difficulty separating because they see that the mother, the primary caregiver, is different from them and they also see the power and status vested in the male figure. This observation makes it easier for male children to separate from their mothers.

Chodorow suggests that both women and men should be active parents.[9] By so doing, sexual inequality is less likely to be reproduced and the ambivalence about the mother's role as well as the psychological dependency relationship between mother and daughter is likely to dissipate.

Rossi counters Chodorow's interpretation of the mother/daughter caregiving and dependency relationship by pointing to the limitations of psychoanalysis. She claims that the biological differences between women and men as well as psychological components cannot be ignored. However, Rossi's analysis does not include economic, political and social factors which may produce and reinforce the caregiving role of the daughter and the dependency of the older mother.

Flax addresses the conflict between the need for nurturance and autonomy in the mother/daughter relationship. She claims that women want both nurturance and autonomy in intimate relationships. Since psychological development takes place within a patriarchal family structure, this is hard to obtain. She supports arguments put forth by Dinnerstein, Chodorow, Eichenbaum and Orbach by claiming that the symbiotic bond between the nurturer (usually mother) and infant provides the basis for security, claiming that female children identify more closely with the mother, just as the mother may identify more closely with the daughter. Given this, in addition to the undervalued role of caregiving in our society, the daughter is likely to experience more internal conflict about the mother and her role than the son.

Eichenbaum and Orbach also see the root of ambivalence and dependency in the mother/daughter relationship as best understood by looking at object relations theory. They claim that the mother's role is to teach the daughter to be a nurturer. This role is internalized and becomes part of the daughter's identity, thus, failure to live up to this role is likely to lower self-esteem. Perhaps as the mother is unconsciously teaching her daughter to give to others she is offering herself as a candidate, preparing her daughter to look after her in her older years.[10]

Rubin claims that it is women's socialization that blocks independence, either overtly or covertly, thus consigning women to a lifetime of conflict around dependence and independence. According to Rubin, women fear independence since it is considered a masculine trait; yet if a woman fails at economic independence she may be committing herself to a life of loneliness and poverty.

Women's potential for economic independence is limited as women do not have either the same career choices or earning power as men. Given this, it is not unusual to find that women are economically dependent on men or on the State. If women are dependent on men for economic survival then one can assume that a certain level of emotional dependence is connected to the need for shelter and food. Fischer claims that most older women (mothers) in the United States do not acknowledge any role change and want "intimacy at a distance." Daughters, however, do not agree. They claim that they must "mother" their mothers. Fischer found that women, whether they are working-class or middle-class, are the kin keepers for their families. She also found that adult daughters are uncomfortable when their frail elderly parent is dependent upon them. She claims that adult children try to please their parents as they are still trying to seek approval. Fischer concludes that "parental caregiving is a quintessential woman's role—like motherhood."[11]

Using object relations theory as a means to explain and understand the complex dependency relationship between mother and daughter in general, and the middle-aged daughter and older mother in particular, provides a basis for discussion, but to focus only on the psychoanalytic explanation can be disempowering. While many of these researchers recommend changes in the household division of labour and promote economic independence for women as a means to change the relationship between mother and daughter, this theory still implies a psychological determinist perspective, thereby making change almost impossible.

Social Construction Theory

Feminist social constructionists look at the social structures contributing to the dependency relationship between mother and daughter. Significant issues include caregiving, the gender division of labour, poverty, economic dependence and income insecurity, the historic role and marginality of elderly people, and social policy that promotes dependence. The research provides an analysis of the caregiving role women experience throughout the various stages of their lives, based on the assumption that they have been socialized to be caregivers and that this work is undervalued, underpaid—or in most cases not paid—and that it is perpetuated by patriarchy and the material conditions of women.[12] Graham claims that women's role as caregiver leads to economic dependence and poverty; yet caregiving defines both women's identity and work in our culture. Aronson suggests that the present gender division has the potential to impose dependency on the carers and cared-for in the following manner:

1) A woman who looks after an elderly family member may have to remove herself from the paid labour force. By doing so, she is likely to become economically dependent on other family members or the State.

2) The elderly family member (mostly women) may be forced to accept this type of care as she may have limited resources and/or live in a community with limited resources; she may thus feel powerless and indebted to her daughter.

Walker also states that caring relationships often create dependency and that it is through social policy that dependency is maintained. According to him, women and elderly people—the majority of whom are women—share a dependency status. Walker claims the following groups of people are likely to be economically and psychologically dependent:

1) People who are not part of the labour force: homemakers, welfare recipients, retired elderly people.

2) People who have physical, social and psychological incapacities.

3) People whose freedom is restricted, such as prisoners and low-mobility elderly adults.

4) People who rely wholly or partially on the State for financial aid.

5) People who are denied subsistence or are restricted to limited income.

Townsend maintains that the dependency of the elderly adult is created by the strong push for early retirement, the legitimation of low income, and the lack of control elderly people have over their lives both in institutions and in the community. However, Smith claims that the structured dependency of elderly people existed before industrial capitalism: historically, elderly people have been socially isolated and removed from the workforce. But Phillipson claims that there is a strong co-relation between structured dependency and capitalism. He claims that the system which values productivity fails to meet the needs of elderly people in four ways:

1) Whenever capitalism is in crisis, it is those who are unemployed and/or forced into retirement who suffer most.

2) Defense spending is greater than spending on health and welfare programmes for older adults.

3) Older adults may find themselves caught between the need for better services and State cutbacks.

4) Elderly people receive inadequate pensions.

In Canada, the population of both women and men over sixty-five has grown but women's life expectancy is greater than that of men. Women also experience greater poverty as they age.[13] As of January 1987, 49.2 percent of elderly people in Canada received the Guaranteed Income Supplement as well as Old Age Security (OAS).[14] According to Statistics Canada (1989), 50 percent of elderly single women live below the low income cut-off whereas 30.7 percent of elderly single men live below the poverty line. In fact, Chappell reviewed the Canadian income security and social welfare programmes for elderly people in the 1970s and noted that the system has not changed much since then. There has been an increase in federal support for the health care system, but at the cost of non-medical programmes such as the expansion of community care and/or the development of any resources which would allow elderly people to remain independent.[15]

Leonard claims that the social construction of dependency can be analyzed by realizing that elderly people are marginal to society and this marginality is compounded by gender, class and race/ethnicity. Leonard also claims that since women are devalued in our society, the elderly woman may be treated with less respect than the elderly man and infantilized by their caregivers in general, and daughters in particular.

I question this assumption, as I believe that because women have been socialized to cater to young children and men, a daughter will be more likely to infantilize her father and will do so with less hostility. It is also assumed in our society that men are unable to "look after" themselves, i.e., it is a woman's job to look after a man. However, I believe that fathers may strongly resist being infantilized as it is also a part of their socialization to be independent. Men may like the nurturing but will still try to maintain as much control as possible.

Elderly mothers may also be infantilized but I believe that the motivation is different. Daughters may resent how mothers nurtured them and thus infantilize their mothers in retaliation. On the other hand, mothers who want others to assume responsibility for them may remain ambivalent about being infantilized.

Social construction theorists challenge the status quo and recommend that structural changes occur if socially constructed dependency roles of women and elderly people are to change. For example, Townsend recommends the following structural changes in order to maximize the independence of elderly adults:

1) Those elderly people who can, should continue to work in the paid labour force.

2) Alternate forms of substantial and productive work should be found.

3) Elderly adults should have higher income.

4) Elderly women and men should have greater control over the place and type of required accommodations and services.

The scope of the social construction perspective is broader and less deterministic than the psychoanalytic perspective. Furthermore, to challenge the status quo and provide recommendations for structural changes can empower older people. If barriers to independence were reduced or removed then the dependency relationship between middle-aged daughters and older mothers could assume a different face.

Critique

While both the object relations and social construction theories attempt to understand the dependency relationship between the mothers and daughters, each theory on its own is problematic. Just as most of the psychoanalytic theorists ignore the social, economic and physical aspects of dependency, many social constructionists do not confront the human need for, and the potential problems arising from, emotional dependency. Both perspectives tend to assume a middle-class white Anglo-Saxon bias, which is not to say that women in other classes and cultures do not assume the main caregiving role first in relation to their children and partner, and then to their parents. But it may not be a universal "truth" that women are either dependent on men or lose self-esteem as they age. In some societies, women gain status as they age and are looked upon as socially valuable even though they are not economically productive or actively reproductive. Some psychoanalytic feminist theorists believe patriarchy to be the root of women's oppression and dependence, whereas the social constructionists believe the root to be both material and ideological.

A comprehensive theory which would incorporate and demonstrate the interrelationship between these perspectives is needed—one which would provide a clear link between patriarchy and material conditions of women as well as a clear link between the internalization of dependence and structural factors. The feminist psychoanalytic perspective and the social construction perspective each contribute valuable insight into gender role expectations and the conflict experienced by women due to these expectations. Frosh presents the argument that psychoanalysis is always politically relevant because it deals with people's experience in the social realm and attempts to provide an understanding of how it becomes personal. Basically, this is one way to understand the "complex interweaving of external factors to the individual with what is experienced as most deeply private and personally formative."[16]

Leonard attempts to explain the relationship between ideology, the formation of personality, and social relationships. In his book *Personality and Ideology,* he struggles with the development of a new paradigm by demonstrating that the existing modes of analysis are necessary but insufficient. His attempt to combine perspectives is a progressive step which could provide a path to a fuller understanding of the dependency relationship between the middle-aged daughter and her elderly mother.

Even though feminists have utilized psychoanalytic theory to reflect women's reality, psychoanalysis fundamentally expresses a man's view of the world. In addition, social policy and social structures also reflect the perceptions of men. However, the feminist adaptation of object relations theory attempts to link a women's psychic structure to women's material reality. Yet even this theory does not go far enough. Still, these perspectives can be used to explain and change social structures and the realities of women as well as men. By using the analyses provided by psychoanalysis and social constructionists, the complex dependency relationship becomes clearer. It is important to realize that elements which influence emotional, economic, social and physical dependence have to be considered in the context of cultural, social and political factors.

Findings and Discussion

In an attempt to interrelate feminist object relations theories and social constructionist perspectives, and to isolate factors which contribute to the dependency relationship, in-depth interviews were carried out with five mothers and their daughters to explore the following questions:

1) Did factors such as limited income, social isolation, early retirement, inadequate housing, and inadequate community support reflect the realities of these older mothers?

2) Could older mothers and their daughters identify barriers to independence?

3) Did these mothers and daughters feel a particular emotional attachment to each other and if, so, how would they describe and explain it?

4) How did older mothers and their daughters feel about their dependency relationship?

5) Did mothers and daughters have any suggestions for change?

Given the limited sample used in this study, one cannot generalize the answers. One can, however, use these findings to support existing research, provide data for policy development and social work practice, and promote structural change.

In this section, it will be shown how the research findings based on the eleven interviews support the assumptions of both theories. The themes of economic, physical, social, and psychological dependence will be addressed.

Economic Dependence

The findings indicate that while the mothers in the sample were not economically dependent, they were aware of the role economics plays in maintaining their independence. They were concerned that their present incomes could diminish, thereby forcing them to rely on their daughters for economic support. That no daughter feared that she might have to financially support her mother is an indication of the mothers' relatively secure financial status. Mothers wished to ensure that they would have sufficient income so that they would not have to rely on, or be a burden to their daughters.

> I always took care of my daughter and myself and I'm not suddenly going to become financially dependent on my daughter. I want to have enough money so that I'll be taken care of without changing my standard of living.

The elderly mothers understood that economic security would allow them to have some control over their lives if they became physically dependent.

> I have to watch my money because I do not want to become a burden to my daughter. I may become physically dependent and I'll need my money to help me maintain my independence as much as possible. I don't want to be a burden.

Most mothers in the sample had never worked in the paid labour force. They had limited or no economic independence while their husbands were alive. Perhaps because they had depended on their spouses for financial support, they understood their position in this arrangement. They may have felt restricted, and believed that they did have the knowledge or the right to make economic decisions which would affect their lives. It seems to me that they understood their own psychological need for economic independence.

Social constructionists, such as Graham, Aronson and Walker claim that while a woman's role as caregiver both defines her identity and work in our culture, this role can lead to economic dependency and poverty. Walker states that people such as homemakers, welfare recipients and retired elderly people who are not part of the labour force are likely to be both economically and psychologically dependent. Leonard explains how this form of dependence is created by the ideology inherent in a patriarchal culture and by the material conditions of women. While the object relations theorists did not overtly look at women's economic dependency, they did, however, look at women's role and position in a patriarchal culture.[17] According to these researchers, caregiving and nurturing are the roles assigned to women—roles that are undervalued and underpaid.

In a materialist society, a person's worth is measured by her ability to produce: if a person is productive, she is rewarded financially. Since a caregiver is not a producer, she usually has to rely on others for economic support which can cause vulnerability and psychological dependence. It is assumed that these mothers were aware of the link between economic and psychological dependency in their marriages, and therefore wanted to resist repeating this type of relationship with their daughters. Perhaps economic independence allows these mothers to feel worthy and that they have control over their lives.

Physical Dependence

All the mothers in the sample feared physical dependence and stressed that they did not want to burden their daughters. They linked their economic status to their ability to maintain some control over their lives if and when they became less able to accomplish daily activities. Most expressed the wish to remain in their homes as long as possible—meaning as long as they had financial resources which would allow them to hire support people. The following are responses by two elderly mothers who expressed this concern.

> I do worry about physical dependence. I don't want to be a burden. Otherwise I am content. I make myself content. I never want to live with my daughter or any of my children. We are two different generations and I'd feel as though I'd be invading their privacy. They won't be able to talk or act as freely when I'm around. I don't think it is just me, it is any parent.

I never want to become dependent on my children, I would rather die than become help-less.

Daughters, on the other hand, feared the potential of their mothers' growing physical dependence. They expressed the fear of an increased workload.

You know if my dad could no longer drive, I guess I'd be called upon to do more chauffeur-ing. I don't like the prospect of it. It is not just an invasion of my time. It is very complex. I feel in-tense about it.

Fischer found that adult daughters are uncomfortable when their frail elderly parents are dependent on them. She believes that adult children are still trying to seek approval from their parents and, therefore, trying to please them.

I just assumed it was my obligation as I grew up in a household in which my grandparents and then my grandmother lived with us. I thought it was the continuation of my role as a good daughter.

This creates ambivalence since, first of all, not only have daughters seen their mothers relegated to this undervalued role, but they too, have been socialized to play the same part.[18] Some women in the sample said that they felt diminished by their mothers' caregiving role and the dependency it created, and thus struggled to resist repeating this same pattern.

Secondly, on a psychic level, daughters have internalized the oppression of the mother/daughter relationship.[19] Considering one of Chodorow's theoretical assumptions that daughters have difficulty separating from mothers, perhaps the dependency relationship between middle-aged daughters and elderly mothers is a continuation of this earlier relationship. Therefore, to assume the physical care of dependent mothers may trigger a psychological reaction in daughters. Daughters may be struggling with, and resisting, their dependence on mothers.

> I don't like to see people totally helpless; I guess it is my fear of being totally helpless. As I said, it is only recently that I've been called upon to provide physical support. I know if my mother ever became physically dependent I could not provide the care. There will have to be institutional care or outside help or some type of structural care. I also know that my mother would not want to burden me with that job. To me this is related not only to her experience as caregiver to my grandmother but to my mother's fear of rejection as well as her concern for politeness and correctness. You know, I just helped a friend move. This person was almost completely helpless yet I did not feel as anxious as I was when I helped my mother move. I guess there is something special

about seeing your mother becoming more frail and dependent.

Social Dependence

While all mothers expressed a wish not to burden their daughters by either calling them too frequently or by placing too many demands on them, this in fact was not the case, since they did rely on their daughters to fulfil their social needs. The following comments were made by three different elderly mothers.

> I enjoy her. I do not pry ... even if I'm lonely. I think once a child is an adult and living on their own, they are entitled to their own life but I do receive and need emotional support from Carol. I like to do things with her.

> Sometimes I feel very lonely and I hate to eat by myself so I try to make myself feel better. Sometimes, when I set the table, I put flowers on it. Sometimes I do not eat so well because I feel so alone, so why bother. My children do ask me out and I wonder if it is because they feel sorry for me but I'd like to believe they really want me with them. I enjoy going out with my children. I prefer to be with them than with my friends.

> I speak to my daughter daily. I do not call her as I know that she is very busy and I do not want to

bother her. I sometimes feel that my daughter's frequent calls are a check to see if I'm still alive. I do feel secure knowing that Judy will call me or that I can call her if I need her. Even though I wonder about her frequent calls I believe she also calls to chat. She does interesting work and not everyone would appreciate what she has to say … but I am her mother. Her business is confidential but she feels safe to share some ideas with me.

In much of the work on aging, there is limited discussion on this form of dependency. Social dependency is believed to be linked to economic and physical dependency. It is frequently assumed that if a mother is financially independent and is physically able, she will have an active social life, but this assumption is problematic because women's assigned role must be analyzed in order to understand their isolation.

Women who assumed the role of family caregiver and did not work in the paid labour force are likely to feel and be isolated. These women were encouraged to define themselves through their household work and their families. Consequently, they learned to rely on husbands—whose labour is external to the household—as a link to the social world. They may also have learned to depend on and live through their children's daily experiences. Therefore, mothers who lived a traditional role may not have established an independent social life. To begin to do so, once one is an elderly woman, is an unrealistic expectation. Four of the five elderly mothers in the sample had never worked outside the household. During their earlier lives they had counted on their husbands and children for social fulfilment. To expect middle-aged daughters to fulfil this need is a continuation of the life-long relationship established between mother and daughter.

Daughters resented and some resisted the role of organizing their mothers' social life. Mothers' social dependency posed a demand on the daughters' time. Daughters had to struggle with competing demands placed on them by husbands, children, elderly mothers and labour force responsibilities. Three daughters made the following comments.

> Sunday is a day for social visits. We also take my mother-in-law … the same day, the same time … they talk to each other and we don't have to entertain them.

> My mother stopped doing her own social activities once she lived with us. As a matter of fact I stopped inviting people over because I resented my mother using my friends as her social outlet. I also found that I wanted to go out and escape the oppression I felt by my mother's presence in my space.

> If I stay home and don't see my mother I feel uncomfortable and I feel better if I see her. I think I feel that way because she is alone. I know my mother depends on me for social fulfilment; maybe she is even emotionally dependent on me.

> I get upset because she won't get actively in-
> volved. I sometimes wonder if her lack of invol-
> vement is a way of getting my attention.

It is also possible that the daughters' resistance was an attempt to set limits both for the present relationship and one which may evolve in the future.

Psychological Dependence

Based on the interviews, it appears that mothers' psychological dependence on daughters is related to current expressed needs of mothers ... that is, social isolation and some physical assistance. However, daughters' psychological dependence on mothers could be related to the early mother/ daughter nurturing relationship. Daughters may not have separated and differentiated from mothers, and therefore depend on their mothers for emotional satisfaction.

> I tend to nurture my mother. I feel rewarded by
> nurturing her ... a need of mine is met. She ac-
> knowledges my nurturing and it is more than
> my children do so I feel good about it. She does
> emotionally support me. It is interesting, at
> times, I consider my mother to be just another
> one of my children ... make them feel good,
> make her feel good; buy for them, buy for her.

The following are comments made by two mothers about their relationship to their daughters.

Mothers and daughters are both feminine and can discuss things together ... things that a mother can't discuss with a son ... just because they are the same sex they understand ... daughters seem to care more ... it is not devotion but understanding.

My daughters are part of me. They provide more caregiving to me than my sons. My sons are closer to their wives' family but they are proud of me and encourage my independence.

Based on sample findings, it appears as though the more socially and psychologically dependent the mother is, the more she is infantilized by her daughter. Some daughters either overtly or covertly infantilized their mothers even though mothers attempted to resist this treatment. One daughter made the following comments about her mother.

It took her all day to peel potatoes for dinner. I gave up and did it myself.

I don't want to be my mother's mother. It seems to me that I have assumed this role long before most of my peers. I don't like to be depended upon like this. I feel choked. Maybe I feel this way because I'm an only child or what is more frightening to me is that I see some of my mother's behaviour in me—like not making a decision. This really scares me.

Yet her mother stated:

I mothered my daughter all my life and I find it difficult to have her mother me. On one hand I feel comforted but on the other hand I can still make decisions and do things for myself ... maybe slower but I can still do it.

Another daughter stated:

You know I can't wait until I turn fifty, then I will join the Golden Age and go on Sundays. My mother will be invited to come with me. I hope she'll come because she thinks that the Golden Age is only for old people. I'll show her. She'll see things and I hope she'll become involved. I suppose my plan with Golden Age is like taking a child to nursery school so in that way I'm treating my mother like a child.

And this daughter's mother claimed the following:

When my daughter checks up on me as frequently as she does I resent it. She is not my mother and I tell her so.

Infantilizing adults encourages them to be dependent and diminishes their self-esteem. Leonard asserts that since women are devalued in a patriarchal culture they are more likely than men to be infantilized.

However, it is also possible that a daughter's infantilization of her mother could be due to her anger toward her mother. She may feel that she was not adequately nurtured as a child or she might be angry that her mother is no longer capable of providing nurturing. The daughter may also resent the neediness created in her by her mother's caregiving. Mothers may also be infantilized by their daughters because they resent their mothers' subordinate role. Daughters may subconsciously want to punish their mothers for not being more empowered role models. In the sample, some daughters felt nurtured by infantilizing their mothers, while others felt vindicated.

> I feel that my mother has always been dependent on me but not in a physical sense, because she always did things for me, but in an emotional sense. She was an "at home mother" and depended upon me to provide her with some *raison d'être* and to fill up her day. On that kind of profound psychic level I feel as though I've done my "caring for" to my mother. I feel as though my mother would be happy to be taken care of and depend on me more. I guess there is a daughter's resistance to be conscripted into this role. I've distanced myself for self-protec-

> tion, because in order to maximize my relation-
> ship with her I had to maximize the extent to
> which I was needy. On one hand, you fulfil a
> neediness within her and she creates a needi-
> ness within you. My mother did less of this
> with my brother as I think that my mother al-
> ways saw my brother as a separate person and I
> think I was more of an extension of her.

Clearly, psychological dependency is a difficult and complex dimension. However, it cannot be understood separately from other forms of dependency. It is important to understand how an individual's psychological make-up is related to ideology. A person internalizes their culture's ideology; thus that ideology has an impact on their psychic structures.

The ideology of a society reflects values and beliefs of that society. In a patriarchal society, women are taught to be mother, housekeeper, kin-keeper, wife and dutiful daughter. They are also taught to be dependent on the men in their lives for financial security. Women internalize these expectations. This helps form the woman's identity and contributes to her self-concept and self-esteem. A culture's ideology thus not only creates dependency roles but also maintains them.

Social policy, which reflects ideology, serves to maintain and perpetuate the status quo. Social policy which keeps women economically vulnerable and which supports the existing sexual division of labour only perpetuates the psychological dependency of women. As stated, the more dependent a person is on others for economic, physical and social support, the greater the psychological dependence.

While women are socialized to be economically and socially dependent, mothers also teach their daughters to be nurturers. By doing so, they may be unconsciously preparing their daughters to look after them in their old age.[20] Daughters, too, may have grown up with a sense of continuity with their mothers, and therefore have trouble differentiating and separating.[21]

The material conditions of women as well as patriarchal ideology, create and maintain the expected roles of women. Middle-aged daughters' and older mothers' dependency relationships are an expression of these expected roles. In order to have the elderly mother and middle-aged daughter dependency relationship change, social policy which is committed to the economic, physical, social and psychological independence of women must be developed. Furthermore, social workers must be sensitive to ideological assumptions that foster the dependency relationship between elderly mothers and their middle-aged daughters.

Implications for Social Policy and Social Work Practice

Economic Dependence

While the mothers in the sample did not have immediate economic problems, they all expressed fear that their present financial resources could diminish. They wanted to ensure that they had sufficient financial security so that they could maintain some control over their lives should they no longer be able to look after themselves. They did not want to live with or burden their daughters.

As they all lived above the Statistics Canada poverty line, the mothers represented a minority of elderly women in Montréal. Though they were not financially dependent, their fear cannot be ignored. They understood the need to protect their capital. If they consumed this capital, they would have to rely only on Old Age Security and the Guaranteed Income Supplement (GIS) for income security, and their standard of living would go from above to below the poverty line. Given this fear, all mothers in the sample expressed the hope that pensions would be adjusted. Many women felt that their present fixed incomes were unfairly taxed, believing that the cost of living is constantly increasing and methods of taxation did not always take this factor into consideration. Recommendations and concerns presented by the women in this sample support policy suggestions made by Walker and Chappell.

Chappell criticizes the Canadian pension system, claiming that it is regressive and ultimately poses a burden on those in the lower middle income range. Chappell states:

> Although Old Age Security payments, Guaranteed Income Supplement and provincial supplements alter the regressivity of C/QPP somewhat, the total package is progressive only at the lower levels. Old age tax exemptions are even less progressive. They provide more savings for those with more money.[22]

Walker states that approximately 90 percent of elderly people in Britain rely on State benefits for all, or part of their incomes. He explains that financial dependency is closely linked to both deprivation and poverty. According to Walker, the poor tend to be more dependent on others.

By Statistics Canada (1990) standards, the low income margin for a single person living in an urban centre stood at $14,155 yet the maximum OAS and GIS a single elderly person received was approximately $8,850.

In order to change women's financial dependence, women's pension benefits must change. Women ought to receive credit for the years they have spent working in the home. Since the CPP/QPP and company pension benefits are related to salaries earned, the implementation of a pay equity policy is urgently needed. Women are less likely than men to be in the paid labour force and those women who are, tend to earn substantially less than men. Therefore, women in general are more likely than men to live below the poverty line and older women in particular are more likely than older men to live below the poverty line. Elderly women must therefore be ensured an income which is above the poverty line, and taxation measures ought not to favour those who are wealthy. It would seem that the entire Canadian old age security programme must be reformulated so that economic independence is ensured in later life.

Physical Dependence

Four of the five mothers in the sample were living on their own, and one was living in a seniors' residence. All these mothers were able to look after their daily needs, yet they all worried about becoming physically dependent. Those living on their own expressed the desire to be able to maintain their independent living arrangements for as long as possible, and if need be, hoped that their homes could be fitted with aids.

They suggested that the transportation system be improved and adjusted to meet the needs of frail elderly women. Buses should be easier to mount, run more frequently, and bus shelters should be heated. They also suggested that there be an expansion of the bus service available for those elderly women who could no longer use regular public transportation. Some mothers claimed that if they were so physically dependent that they could no longer look after themselves, they wished to at least receive help in their own homes. Finally, all the mothers stated that they did not want to burden their daughters. They wanted to ensure that their financial situation would allow them to have some control over their lives if and when they became physically dependent.

The fact that these mothers wish to live independently supports the research done by the National Advisory Council on Aging. Nonetheless, many people who work with frail elderly women enhance their dependence rather than encourage and promote their independence. This situation existed among some of the mother/daughter pairs in the sample, for example, one daughter would not wait the time it took her mother to peel potatoes. She did it herself. With this action and attitude, the daughter encouraged her mother's dependence.

Given that most of the mothers in the sample wished to maintain an independent living arrangement for as long as possible, they would be encouraged by some of the recommendations made by Walker and the National Advisory Council on Aging. Walker notes that if a severely disabled elderly person is living in an accommodation which is adapted to meet her physical needs, then she might not become dependent on others for care. As an example, the height of kitchen counters could be adjusted to accommodate wheelchairs. Not to allow for this type of adjustment demonstrates how structures create and maintain the dependence of elderly women.

The National Advisory Council on Aging has made a number of recommendations that would promote some form of independent living for those elderly people who have health problems requiring lifestyle adjustments. Their recommendations are meant for the general elderly population; however, since older women are more likely than older men to be placed in long-term care institutions, they would benefit most. The National Advisory Council on Aging recommends that:

1) Those who plan and provide services to elderly people have as the goal of their activities the promotion of independence of elderly people.

2) Elderly people should be made aware of their rights with regard to independent living.

3) Access to affordable assistance devices and follow-up services should be provided to ensure that elderly people are using the necessary devices properly.

4) Elderly people ought to have a right to choose to live "at risk" if they are found to be mentally competent by professional standards.

5) For those elderly people who are suffering from sensory losses and/or other physical disabilities and living with a family member, counselling should be provided to help both the elderly person and her caregiver. These caregivers ought to be trained to promote as much independence as possible.[23]

A further impediment to independent living is the general lack of community support. While we may be committed to deinstitutionalization as a policy, community support services are limited and underfunded. Lack of these services may force frail elderly mothers to move into institutions, whereas these women could possibly still live on their own if adequate community support were provided. At the moment, in Québec, there are 127 day centres structured to meet the needs of frail elderly people.[24]

To maintain elderly women's physical independence, community-based support systems must be available on a twenty-four hour, seven day basis. Both formal and informal community-based services should be available to provide a continuum of care in accordance with the changing needs of the individual senior.[25] Furthermore, in order to ensure that policy meets the needs of elderly women who are physically dependent, this target population should be consulted and integrated into policy planning teams.

Clearly, if elderly women are to maintain independence, major policy changes must occur. If this were so, some of the fears expressed by elderly mothers in the sample could be alleviated.

Social Work Practice Implications and Social and Psychological Dependence

Social Dependence

Although there seem to be many recreation and social action groups organized for or by older women, social isolation for many elderly women appears to be a problem. As already noted, most mothers in the sample expressed feelings of loneliness and looked to their daughters to fill this void. Daughters resented their mother's dependence on them for social fulfilment. In fact, it was in this area of social fulfilment that the dependency relationship was found to manifest itself most. These findings lead one to believe that these elderly women may have found it difficult to establish social relations outside the family. They may have led isolated lives as family care-providers, may have defined themselves through social relations within the family, and may have been taught that offspring are expected to fulfil parental social needs. How can one be expected to alter these patterns at seventy-five if reliance on the family has been a lifelong expectation?

It is also possible that the recreational programmes that are available did not meet the social needs of the mothers in the sample. Sometimes programmes are created without consulting the very population they are intended to serve. The programmes and/or the workers reflect an ageist attitude, so common in our culture. Programmes planned for this population can be uninteresting, repetitive and boring. Some workers, also, tend to treat elderly women as though they are incapable of making decisions for themselves. Consequently, even more so than elderly men, they are treated like children.[26] If mothers in the sample resented and resisted being infantilized by their daughters, they might possibly refuse to become involved with any person and/or programme which attempts to do the same.

Social workers should be aware of such structures that encourage dependency, and attempt to empower both mother and daughter instead. In this way, each would be supported in gaining more control over their lives. Mothers would be encouraged to talk about their feelings of isolation and loneliness. Their ideas regarding social programming would be solicited and could then be used to help develop programmes of interest to them. To reduce social dependency, it is important that elderly women who are dependent on their daughters for social fulfilment be encouraged to develop skills that would allow them to establish a social life separate from their daughters. Forming networks and building relationships with other older women who share interests could reduce social dependence on daughters and provide support for mothers.

Daughters should be encouraged to talk about the pressure they feel from the additional burden of entertaining their mothers and, in a supportive environment, be made to understand how they, perhaps, contribute to the situation. Subsequently, daughters would be encouraged to talk about changes they would like to see, and set clear limits with their mothers so that they could feel less resentful. They would also be encouraged to talk to their peers, thereby reducing some of the stress they experience. These women could also help each other to change the negative aspects of their relationships with their mothers.

Both mothers and daughters would be encouraged to understand that the nature of mother/daughter relationships is socially constructed and related to the ascribed role of women in a patriarchal culture. To do this would generalize the problem and, at the same time, demonstrate how private problems are really public issues.

Psychological Dependence

The root of psychological dependency begins in infancy and evolves over one's life. Psychological dependence, within limitations, is believed to be a healthy human need,[27] however, one should question this form of dependency when it becomes destructive.

In the sample, mothers who were infantilized by their daughters resented and tried to resist this treatment. To infantilize a person can erode her self-esteem and feelings of self-worth. Women in general, and older women in particular, are valued less than younger and older men, which usually means being treated with less respect.

As a social worker, one could help daughters to understand that by infantilizing mothers they are contributing to their mothers' dependency. It should also be noted that infantilization of the mother could be a possible expression of anger. One would then encourage daughters to talk about their possible anger towards their mothers. Clearly, one would try to do this without invoking unnecessary feelings of guilt. Finally, this behaviour could be looked at in relationship to the sexual division of labour. Chodorow and Eichenbaum and Orbach claim that only when men assume a more nurturing role and share household duties will the nature of the mother/daughter psychological dependency relationship change. Women must also have the opportunity to receive equal pay for comparable work. Once women's work is recognized and rewarded in the same way as men's, their status changes.

To situate the mother/daughter dependency relationship in the context of the social structure could empower both mother and daughter. They might then understand that their particular relationship is a reflection of, and response to, values in patriarchal culture and the material conditions of women. By presenting these ideas, mothers and daughters could learn that their dependency relationship is not unique to them, but is a symptom of a larger social problem which they have some power to change.

Summary and Conclusion

My research findings support the work done by feminist object relations and social construction theorists. The former explains this relationship in psychological terms, believing that the root of the mother/daughter dependency relationship in a patriarchal culture begins with early nurturing experiences between the caregiver—mother and infant. This relationship is socially constructed as women are assigned the caregiving role. According to the social constructionists, the dependency relationship between an elderly mother and middle-aged daughter is created by interaction between patriarchy and economic structures. Ideologies common to both patriarchy and capitalism produce and reproduce the status quo. Peace claims that:

> the underlying ideologies of both patriarchy and capitalism with their emphasis on male power and male domination, have culminated in the use of the family and women's traditional role within it as a controlling vehicle for reproducing the status quo and reinforcing social inequalities.[28]

Developing and implementing policy that will challenge the status quo is a difficult task, but it can be done. Only when social policies and peoples' behaviours and attitudes change could there be a change in the dependency relationship between the middle-aged daughter and her mother. In the meantime, social workers can learn to be sensitive to the nature of this particular relationship. They must work towards empowering mothers and daughters with skills to resist being conscripted into roles they may not want.

Since values, beliefs, cultural norms and economic insecurity may influence the mother/daughter dependency relationship, other ethnic and class groupings must also be studied in order to further refine this research. Clearly, the social structures that establish and perpetuate dependency relationships between elderly mothers and middle-aged daughters ought to be challenged. To understand the structures that create and perpetuate this dependency relationship will heighten social workers' sensitivity and contribute to the nature of social work practice in gerontology. Further, unravelling the complexities of the mother/daughter dependency relationship will ultimately empower all those involved.

Notes

1. Understanding Seniors' Independence, May 1989.
2. Beland 1987.
3. Brody 1985.
4. Canada 1986, Canada's Seniors: A Dynamic Force.
5. Horowitz 1985.
6. Frosh 1987, p. 273.
7. Ernst 1987.
8. Chodorow 1987.
9. Ibid.
10. Eichenbaum and Orbach 1988, 1987, 1983.
11. Fischer 1986, p. 194.
12. Arcana 1979; Aronson 1988, 1986, 1985; Brody 1985; Cantor 1983; Doress and Siegal 1987; Finch 1984; Finch and Groves 1982; Gee and Kimball 1987; Heller 1986; Horowitz 1985.
13. Gee and Kimball 1987.
14. Marshall, D. 1987.
15. Chappell 1987.
16. Frosh, p. 269.
17. Chodorow 1989, 1987, 1978a, 1978b; Flax 1981; Rubin 1983, 1979.
18. Chodorow 1989, 1987, 1978a, 1978b; Eichenbaum and Orbach 1988, 1987, 1983; Ernst 1987; Flax 1981; Fischer 1986; Rubin 1983, 1979.
19. Chodorow 1989, 1987, 1978a, 1978b.
20. Eichenbaum and Orbach 1988, 1987, 1983.
21. Chodorow 1989, 1987, 1978a, 1978b.
22. Chappell, p. 495.

23. Understanding Seniors' Independence 1989, pp. 38-42.
24. Johnston 1989.
25. National Advisory Council on Aging 1989.
26. Leonard 1985.
27. Eichenbaum and Orbach 1983; Rubin 1983; 1979.
28. Peace 1986, p. 65.

References

Arcana, Judith. (1979). *Our Mothers' Daughters.* Berkeley: Shameless Hussy Press.

Aronson, Jane. (1985). "Family care of the elderly: Underlying assumptions and their consequences." *The Canadian Journal of Aging.* Vol. 4, No. 3, pp. 115-125.

_____ (1986). "Care of the frail elderly. Whose crisis? Whose responsibility?" Paper presented at the Canadian Association of Schools of Social Work Conference. Winnipeg, June, 1986.

_____ (1988). "Women's experience in giving and receiving care: Pathways to social change." Unpublished doctoral thesis. University of Toronto.

Beland, F. (1987). "Multigenerational households in a contemporary perspective." *The International Journal of Aging and Human Development.* Vol. 25, No. 2, pp. 147-166.

Brody, E. (1985). "Parent care as a normative family stress." *The Gerontologist.* Vol. 25, No. 1, pp. 19-29.

Canada. (1986). *Canada's Seniors: A Dynamic Force.* Ottawa.

Canada. Statistics Canada. (1989). *Income Distribution by Size in Canada.* Catalogue 13-207.

Canada. Statistics Canada. (1990). *Income Distribution by Size in Canada.* Catalogue 13-207.

Canada. National Advisory Council on Aging. (1989). *Understanding Seniors' Independence. Report No. 1: The Barriers and Suggestions for Action.* Ottawa.

Cantor, M. (1983). "Strain among caregivers: A study of experience in the United States." *The Gerontologist.* Vol. 23, No. 6, pp. 597-604.

Chappell, N. (1987). "Canadian Income and Health-Care Policy: Implications for the elderly." In *Aging in Canada. Social Perspectives.* Edited by V. Marshall. Toronto: Fitzhenry and Whiteside.

Chodorow, Nancy, (1978a). "Mothering object relations and the female oedipal configuration." *Feminist Studies.* Feb., Vol. 4, No. 1, pp. 137-158.

_____ (1978b). *The Reproduction of Mothering: Psychoanalysis and the Sociology of Gender.* Berkeley: University of California Press.

_____ (1987). "Feminism and difference: Gender, relation, and psychoanalytic perspective." In *The Psychology of Women: Ongoing Debates.* Edited by M. Walsh. New Haven: Yale University Press, pp. 249-264.

_____ (1989). "Family structure and feminine personality." Reprinted from *Women, Culture and Society,* (1974). In *Feminist Frontiers: Rethinking Sex, Gender and Society.* Edited by l. Richardson and V. Taylor. New York: Random House, pp. 43-58.

Dinnerstein, Dorothy. (1976). *The Mermaid and the Minotaur: Sexual Arrangements and Human Malaise.* New York: Harper Colopan Books.

Doress, Paula and Diane Laskin Siegal in co-operation with the Boston Women's Health Collective. (1987). *Ourselves, Growing Older. Women Aging with Knowledge and Power.* Toronto: A Touchstone Book. Simon and Schuster.

Eichenbaum, Luise and Susie Orbach. (1983). *What Do Women Want? Exploding the Myth of Dependency.* New York: Berkeley Publishing Group.

_____ (1988). *Between Women: Love, Envy and Competition in Women's Friendship.* New York: Viking Press.

Ernst, S. (1987). "Can a daughter be a woman? Women's identity and separation." In *Living with the Sphinx-Papers from the Women's Therapy Centre.* Edited by S. Ernst and M. Maguire. London: The Women's Press Ltd., pp. 68-115.

Finch, Janet. (1984). "Community care: Developing non-sexist alternatives." *Critical Social Policy.* Vol. 9, pp. 6-18.

Finch, Janet and Dulcie Groves. (1982). "By women for women: Caring for the frail elderly." *Women's Studies International Forum.* Vol. 5, No. 5, pp. 427-438.

Flax, J. (1981). "The conflict between nurturance and autonomy in mother-daughter relationships and within feminism." In *Women and Mental Health.* Edited by E. Howell and M. Bayes. New York: Basic Books, pp. 53-69.

Fischer, Lucy Rose. (1986). *Linked Lives. Adult Daughters and Their Mothers.* New York: Harper & Row Publishers.

Frosh, Stephen. (1987). *The Politics of Psychoanalysis.* London: Macmillan.

Gee, Ellen M. and Meredith M. Kimball. (1987). *Women and Aging.* Toronto: Butterworth.

Graham, H. (1983). "Caring a labour of love." In *A Labour of Love: Women, Work and Caring.* Edited by J. Finch and D. Groves. London: Routledge and Kegan Paul, pp. 13-30.

Heller, Anita F. (1986). *Health and Home: Women as Health Guardians.* Ottawa: Canadian Advisory Council on the Status of Women.

Horowitz, Amy. (1985). "Sons and daughters as caregivers to older parents: Differences in role performance and consequences." *The Gerontologist.* Vol. 25, No. 6, pp. 612-617.

Johnston, David. (1989). "Independence for the elderly." *The Gazette.* Montréal: Sunday, December 3.

Leonard, Peter (1985). *Personality and Ideology: Towards a Materialist Understanding of the Individual.* London: Macmillan Educational Ltd.

Leonard, P. (1987). "Dependency, Gender and Class in Old Age." Paper presented at the 55th Congress of Association Canadienne-Française pour l'avancement des Sciences. University of Ottawa. May 1987.

Marshall, Doris. (1987). *Silver Threads: Critical Reflections on Growing Old.* Toronto: Between the Lines.

Peace, S. (1986). "The forgotten female: Social policy and older women." In *Aging and Social Policy: A Critical Assessment.* Edited by C. Phillipson and A. Walker. London: Gower Publishers, pp. 61-86.

Phillipson, C. (1982). *Capitalism and the Construction of Old Age.* London: Macmillan.

Rossi, A. (1987). "On the reproduction of mothering: A methodological debate." In *The Psychology of Women: Ongoing Debates.* Edited by M. Walsh. New Haven: Yale University Press, pp. 265-273.

_____ (1989). "Gender and parenthood: An evolutionary perspective." In *Feminist Frontiers: Rethinking Sex, Gender and Society.* Edited by L. Richardson and V. Taylor. New York: Random House, pp. 102-110.

Rubin, Lillian B. (1979). *Women of a Certain Age: The Midlife Search for Self.* New York: Harper & Row Publishers.

_____ (1983). *Intimate Strangers: Men and Women Together.* New York: Harper & Row Publishers.

Smith, R. (1984). "The structured dependence of the elderly as a recent development: Some sceptical historical thoughts." *Aging and Society.* Vol. 4, No. 4, pp. 409-428.

Townsend, P. (1981). "The structural dependence of the elderly: A creation of social policy in the twentieth century." *Aging and Society.* Vol. 1, No. 1.

Walker, A. (1982). "Dependency and old age." *Social Policy and Administration.* Vol. 16, No. 2, pp. 115-135.

Walker, Alan. (1983). "Care for elderly people: A conflict between women and the state." In *A Labour of Love: Women, Work and Caring.* Edited by J. Finch and D. Groves. London: Routledge and Kegan Paul, pp. 106-128.

3

The Experience of Italian Women

Rita Bonar

Introduction

The experience of aging is both a social and psychological process which can only be examined and properly understood vis-à-vis other individuals. It is not a passive experience but active, where individuals participate in creating their life histories.[1] This is no less true of aged women receiving care than it is of any other age group; however, as a research focus it has been greatly neglected.

During the past ten years, both feminist and gerontological studies have focused on the issue of the caregiving role in families, particularly on women providing care for their aged relatives. An imbalanced understanding of the issues involved in a caring relationship[2] has thus been created, since the stress and strain that caregiving can exert on those who take responsibility for their aged family members have been extensively documented, but the socio-psychological realities of aged care-receivers themselves have been less thoroughly examined.[3] Some feminist and gerontological studies have corrected this imbalance by drawing attention to the issue of care-receiving and its impact on the well-being of aged women recipients.[4] One limitation of this more recent research is that the focus has been on documenting the perceptions of middle-class, English-speaking women such that ethnicity and working-class status are rarely addressed.

In recent years, research in Québec has favoured in-depth studies of issues facing the aged female population.[5] A significant proportion of these women suffer from multiple chronic illnesses. Studies show the connection between social and economic issues and how these women experience their health problems.[6] Often these women are without a spouse to care for them and are more dependent on other family members for care. In addition, a major government study, the Rochon Commission, argued for the need for future studies to reflect an understanding of the various ethnic groups in Québec society.

The combination of the above-mentioned issues influenced the focus of this research study: women living in Québec who are over sixty-five years of age, of ethnic background, in frail or poor health, and are receiving care from family members. Among ethnic groups, Italian women were selected. Italians currently rank as the third largest ethnic group in Québec and the fourth largest in Canada.[7] Demographic analyses indicate that on the whole the Canadian-Italian population is a young one, with just 6.7 percent over the age of sixty-five; but in Montréal, Québec, this percentage rises to 7.9 percent. This ratio of young to old, as well as deeply entrenched cultural expectations, may account for the fact that chronically-ill Italian women are more likely to receive care from family members, their primary supporters.[8]

A main assumption of this essay is that aged women actively participate in creating their life histories. Their present experience as care-receivers continues to be shaped by socially relevant factors such as their gender, social class, and ethnicity. As well, the nature of their primary social supporters further influences specific social and psychological aspects of their well-being. Therefore, the perceptions of aged Italian women receiving care are examined in this study by discussing their experiences from a feminist theoretical perspective which maintains that the experiences of these women are important and need to be documented. Since no event or social fact can be understood outside its context, all social events are interconnected and behaviour happens between people rather than inside people.[9]

Data and Methodology

The data on which this analysis is based were obtained from sixty-one interviews with thirty participants over the age of sixty-five. Participants were interviewed in their treatment environments (i.e. hospital, day centre, senior centre) with follow-up interviews conducted in their home setting. As a general rule, the more serious the chronic condition, the more interviews were needed to collect the same amount of information. Of the thirty participants who initially consented to participate, three were forced to withdraw due to serious health crises. The interviews with the rest of the twenty-seven participants were accomplished in full and constituted the sample size.

The Italian Women Interviewed

The twenty-seven aged Italian participants can be described as being of the same generation, all born between 1903 and 1922, and ranging in age from sixty-eight to eighty-seven years. For purposes of this study, these women have been subdivided into two groups, one the *Italian-Immigrant group*, the other the *Italian-Canadian group*. The first group includes fourteen women who were born in Italy and immigrated to Canada in adulthood after the Second World War, between 1955 and 1965. Also included in this group is one woman who immigrated in 1980. Of the second group, Italian-Canadians, eight participants were born in Montréal and four were born in Italy but immigrated before age eleven, and attended at least elementary schooling in Montréal.

The sociodemographic characteristics of these women provide an appreciation for individual differences and identify common patterns among the participants. Most of the women interviewed had been married. Six women were still married when interviewed; seventeen were widowed; one was divorced; and one was separated. Two of the women had never married. All of the participants identified themselves as Roman Catholic.

In terms of class, three elements of these participants' socioeconomic status were considered: education, occupation, and financial situation. Eight women of the immigrant group had never attended school; the other seven attended only elementary school, ranging from grade 1 to grade 6. However, the education level of the Italian-Canadian participants was markedly higher. All participants in this group had attended school, ranging from grade 3 to university. The language spoken among the Italian-Immigrant group was predominantly Italian whereas the Italian-Canadian women were all fluent in English, French, and Italian.

For those who had worked outside the home, occupations held by the participants varied. The Italian-Immigrant women had mainly worked in factories while most Italian-Canadian women had been employed as clerical workers. For both groups, the reason given for working was to supplement their spouses' incomes. When asked about their financial situations, nine women of the Italian-Immigrant group explained that they received financial assistance from their primary supporters, whereas the other six women stated that their savings and pensions were sufficient for their needs. Eight women of the Italian-Canadian group informed me that they owned their own homes and had sufficient savings to meet their present needs. The other women explained that they are currently renting their homes but still had no serious financial worries. Hence, the Italian-Canadian women appeared generally to be more financially secure than the Italian-Immigrant women.

The accounts of the twenty-seven women interviewed addressed the study's general areas of questioning: a) key elements of the participants' life histories (i.e. identifying information, family history, major life events); b) current situations (i.e. chronic illness(es), primary social supporters, history of care-receiving, financial situation, psychosocial disposition); c) perceptions of themselves as aged Italian women (i.e. key events in family and work history, constraints experienced involving gender, class, and ethnicity issues, present needs); d) perceptions about their primary social supporters; and e) perceptions about being a care-receiver.

The Experience of Aged Italian Women

Past studies of aged Italian immigrants stress that a female's life career was fulfilled as she went from her father's household to that of her husband to that of her son.[10] Studies of second-generation Italian women imply that they simply moved from their father's household to that of their husband, to that of their daughter or daughter-in-law.[11] However, a more accurate rendering of the pattern would be: as a female, each of these women moved through various stages in her life. She was first a child, an apprentice in womanhood. Upon her marriage, she was a responsible woman who fulfilled economic and family roles. In motherhood and old age, she progressively became more a role model of womanhood to her daughters, daughters-in-law, nieces, goddaughters, and grandchildren.[12]

This section focuses on the experiences of these aged Italian women as they moved through specific periods in their lives, departing from traditional prescribed roles and searching for greater personal freedom and enhanced status.

It also explores the changes in status these women have had to confront as a result of their chronic illness(es) and from being care-receivers.

The twenty-seven women were encouraged through their socialization processes to be passive, submissive, and subordinate. In fact, "dependency" was considered to be a much valued attribute and the main criterion for becoming a good wife and mother. However, this notion of "dependency" is paradoxical because these roles of wife and mother require strengths.[13] The women were well aware of this contradiction and when asked to identify the best period in their life, they identified the following:

> The best time in my life was before I married. I had no responsibilities. I worried about nothing. After, I had to care for my husband, my children, the house and even go out to work!

Twenty-five of the twenty-seven participants have spent an extended portion of their adult lives in the traditional roles of housewife and mother, a role which cannot be adequately performed by dependent, passive women.[14] These women performed many different functions as nurturers, workers, financial managers, volunteers, and confidantes. They developed many varied skills and resources to ensure the physical and emotional stability of their family units in Canadian society. Hence, their roles and their self-concept as women never matched the "traditional" concepts assigned to them.

Seventeen women (eight out of fifteen Italian-Immigrant women and nine out of twelve Italian-Canadian women) responded in similar fashion when asked: "What obligations, restrictions, difficulties have you experienced because you are a woman?"

> I don't think I was restricted or anything because I was a woman. I don't think it would have mattered. Not in my case, anyway.

> Obligations. Difficulties. I think that I never had any problems because I was a woman. I could do what I wanted. My husband always trusted my judgement in matters. We were a team. Even now, I'm doing what I wanted to do. Of course, I'm restricted because of my health, not because I'm a woman.

These women have abandoned whatever dependence they may have had on their husbands and have transcended certain confines of their sex roles to encompass varying degrees of assertiveness, self-confidence, and autonomy in their everyday existence. The data of this study support the argument that, in spite of tremendous constraints, these women have gained or reaped many benefits.

Certain studies have argued that immigrant women are the recipients of multiple negative statuses, stating that membership in two or more groups which are negatively evaluated can have cumulative effects.[15] Thus, Italian immigrant women can be doubly or triply disadvantaged by virtue of being female and foreign-born, or, female, foreign-born, and from a given country of origin. Furthermore, it has been argued that the situation of these women has added one type of subordination to another.[16] The new economic role as wage-earner is often coupled with the traditional household and mother role.

However, an opposing argument can also be presented—migration implies emancipation. This assessment is based primarily on the view that rural life provides more restrictions for women than for men. Several writers have discussed: 1) the emerging independence of immigrant women as a consequence of their increasingly important economic contributions to the support of the immigrant family; and 2) the superior wage-earning opportunities for some immigrant women which then increase their claims to power and respect in relation to their husbands, and give them more independence.[17]

How do we reconcile these opposing arguments about the double and triple oppression with the emancipating effects of migration? Several studies have argued the importance of emphasizing the perceptions of the immigrant women themselves.[18] One woman stated:

> I worked a lot on the land in Italy from early morning to late at night. I never saw a penny for my work. Here, I worked also but I received money ... I bought things for the children ... for the house ... After work, before going home, my

friend and I always went to the coffee shop for a
doughnut and coffee ...

An increasing amount of literature addresses the question
of whether migration leads to a loss or gain in the status of
women as a result of changes in the distribution of power in
the family.[19] The answers vary. The data from this research
study demonstrate that in most situations the women do
enjoy improved access to and control of economic resources
and hence participate more in the decision-making processes
within the family. However, in a few specific circumstances,
their role in the family has been undermined, especially for
the non-working women who are isolated from an extended
family network and who find themselves increasingly dependent on children to deal with a non-domestic world
where they do not even know the language.

The Italian-Canadian women have reaped, indirectly, the
emancipating effects of migration. They benefited from the
labours of their forerunners—those Italian immigrant
women who contributed to the enhanced status of their
families and of themselves by immigrating to Canada and
struggling to establish themselves economically and socially.
For the Italian-Canadians, the assimilation process was also
eased by their education and accompanying occupational
opportunities.

In general, middle age for these women introduced an increased sense of personal freedom and enhanced status.
Reduced pressure from demanding and, at times, conflicting
roles; fewer restrictions; the right to exert authority over fami-

ly members; satisfaction with their past performance as housewife and mother; and opportunities for achievement and recognition beyond the household, contribute to a relatively high degree of satisfaction in later years.

During the interviews, these women reflected on their middle-aged years, and expressed a certain freedom from responsibilities for their domestic domain when their adult offspring left home to establish their own homes. With this freedom came the search for ways to redefine their lives so that there was minimal discontinuity. In some cases, these women no longer defined their existence primarily in terms of "the man" and "the children" in their lives.

> I was forty-eight years old when we set up the grocery/restaurant business. I maintained it for sixteen years.
>
> (Italian-Immigrant)

> I enjoyed going to concerts. I used to leave my husband home and I went with my friends ... The children were all grown up at that time.
>
> (Italian-Canadian)

Several women enjoyed more leisure activities, especially travel.

> I used to travel with my friends, in a group, to Florida. My husband came, but he hated to come.
>
> (Italian-Immigrant)

> He doesn't like travelling and I did. I've been to
> Europe many times. Always with a friend ...
> never with him.
>
> (Italian-Canadian)

Another activity that many pursued was volunteer work in church organizations or golden age associations.

> My group ... I've been in charge of the choir for a
> long time.
>
> (Italian-Canadian)

> Too many years I visited the sick in the hospital
> with other women.
>
> (Italian-Immigrant)

In certain situations, a woman's access to and control of economic resources were viewed as the basis for her enhanced status and autonomy within the family. These women contributed to decision-making in the family.

> I always paid the expenses for my family. My
> money was for the groceries and other things we
> need and he paid for the house.
>
> (Italian-Immigrant)

> My husband and I always discussed how we
> were going to spend.
>
> (Italian-Canadian)

For other women, being a mother-in-law and/or grandmother was associated with enhanced status.

> My children have done well. They have nice homes, good wives, and healthy children. I have four grandchildren! I am fortunate!
>
> (Italian-Immigrant)

> My children, my grandchildren, and great grandchildren, they always made me what I am—Proud!
>
> (Italian-Canadian)

Food, for some of these women, was used to create and reinforce interpersonal relationships. Feelings of satisfaction and fulfilment were expressed in their description of family meals.

> It [Sunday meal] has always been over at my house. I made the meals for the nine of us. Whenever we would get together it was in my house, and I cooked the meals.
>
> (Italian-Immigrant)

> On Sunday, every Sunday, my sons and their families came and I prepared the meals. I would make their favourite. They looked forward to having the pasta and I enjoyed making it.
>
> (Italian-Canadian)

In general, women from both sample groups of the research expressed a greater focus on their own personal interests and pursuits beginning in midlife. Self-awareness and self-improvement were concepts expressed by participants in both groups, but with greater frequency by the Italian-Canadian women.

Advanced age and chronic illness(es) have affected the status of these women. One woman summarized the experience of being an aged Italian woman suffering from chronic illness as follows:

> I feel like any other aged woman. It is not like in the past years (laugh) ... Some people are so much alone but I have my family, my friends. For some, it is very difficult ... they are always depressed ... I am depressed ... sometimes ... I'm half a woman ... I'm not a healthy woman. I can't do what I used to do. I have to ask or wait for someone to help me.

These women identified their change of status as moving from being an active participant to being a disabled and at times "handicapped" individual. Their relationships with their primary support systems have been affected. Many of the changes are part of a less obvious but more widespread shift in the balance of power in their families. These women, who have supported others throughout their lives, are now the supported. These women who once made the decisions are now told what to do. This transition is a difficult one.

Most of these women had multiple chronic diseases. A total of twenty-one different health problems were reported. Furthermore, they were located through their treatment environments, which means that their illnesses had required medical intervention.

Specific sociocultural factors were evident in relation to incidence and severity of chronic illness(es). In general, the onset and prevalence of disability were more evident among the Italian-Immigrant women than among the Italian-Canadian women, since the former group had also experienced lower socioeconomic and educational status throughout their lives.

However, the perceived severity of their illnesses varied among the women. For some, illness was a relatively minor problem, while others suffered extremely limited mobility and severe pain. In order to understand what it means to live with an illness and the ways in which chronic illnesses are incorporated into one's life, it is necessary to approach the phenomenon as a process involving the individual's ongoing formation and reformation of her self-image and the consequent impact on her self-esteem.[20]

The major challenge for these women focused on their ability to redefine their self-image. Of the two groups, the Italian-Immigrant women had greater difficulty reinterpreting their meaning of self, independent of any roles that they had acquired throughout their lives. Their self-concept had been based on their own social roles and others' expectations; hence, the role losses they experienced had a particularly significant impact on their self-esteem.

I worked all my life. I was a hard worker. I am not what you see today. I raised four children. I made their clothes. I kept them clean. I worked in my husband's business. I helped him. I kept a good home, a clean home. One day, a woman asked me how I managed to care for my family the way I did … they were all well-groomed. What can I say? I was active. I made the most of the time I had from morning to night. But then, I became sick … but only later in my life. My life then changed. Well, I sacrificed throughout my life. My life has been one sacrifice after another.

I'm not worth much … I'm no longer useful … I used to be a wife, a mother, a worker … Now what am I? I'm no longer a wife … my children are all grown up and have left home … I can no longer work because of my paralysis! What is left of me? (cries).

In contrast, several women in the Italian-Canadian group focused more on their personal perceptions regarding abilities and skills. They appeared to rely less on external reactions for reinforcement. They appeared also to be more accepting of the aging process, its limitations, and possibilities. Their self-worth was expressed independent of any roles which they had played throughout their lives.

I'm aging naturally … illness comes with age … I adjust. I still make the decisions. I'm adapting as I go along.

If I see that it's getting that bad, I just take off and go to a doctor, and try to do something about it … complaining about it doesn't help.

Data from both groups of women suggest the fact that an individual's self-image develops throughout the life course, through social experiences with other people in the domestic and public spheres. By the time a person becomes aged, she has constructed a sense of self which has been formulated over time and in response to the views of others and society in general.

Being a Care-Receiver: The Struggle to Remain Independent

These women were chronically ill and had made certain adjustments in their daily lives so that their needs could be met. The most frequently mentioned adjustment was accepting help from someone among their primary social supporters on a regular basis. Twenty-six of the women shared accommodations with their primary social supporters. All twenty-seven women were care-receivers.

These women were themselves caregivers for a considerable part of their life course. They devoted a significant part of their working lives to attending to the needs of young children, ailing relatives and, in some cases, ailing spouses. Many of these women, by midlife, had established a strong sense of personal autonomy in their daily lives. The onset of chronic illness and their subsequent need for increasing support in activities of daily living placed the midlife independence of these women at risk. In terms of their daily life experiences, these care-receivers identified two major constraints on their personal autonomy: physical disabilities engendered by chronic illness and the consequent need to share households in order for care-receiving arrangements to continue. The amount of time for which they had been receiving care ranged from two months to twenty-three years; and the number of years they had shared household living arrangements was between one week and twenty-three years. The participants identified their main caregivers as one or several of the following: spouse, daughter, son, daughter-in-law, son-in-law, sibling, friend, and/or grandchild.

Several studies have reported that persons with chronic disabilities define the limitations imposed by their condition as the greatest impediment to their continued autonomy, and the availability of family help as their greatest resource.[21] However, regarding the latter, some studies have also illustrated the restricting aspects of the relationship between care-receiver and caregiver.[22] For example, Noelker and Poulshock found that 55 percent of the six hundred aged individuals studied complained that the caregivers did too much, and 30 percent reported that their relationship with the caregivers made them feel useless.[23] Talbott's study further argues that the aged mother-adult child caring relationship may be characterized by a power differential, so that some aged mothers feel subordinate to their adult children.[24]

Sharing a household was identified as a threat to their independence since the home has traditionally been considered a woman's world and because there could be many points of potential conflict between members of the two, and at times, three generations. In sharing a household, several issues were mentioned as further restrictions on their independence, such as limitations of personal space and of decision-making.

> I've been living on my own all this time, but now I can't. I need assistance. My son and his family are very good to me. They want me to stay with them. They have wanted me to stay with them before, but I like being on my own. I have a duplex. I have tenants upstairs. I have five and a half rooms to myself. I have always been on my own. Now I can't return home … He has young children. I love them and they love me, but often we argue. I don't think it is a good idea, but the choice is not for me to make.
>
> (Italian-Immigrant)

> When my husband died, I wanted to sell the house, but the children talked and said to me that it is better that I stay in the house and my daughter, this is the youngest daughter, with her family, come and live with me since she was renting. As you can see, it is tight. They have a lot of

furniture. They say I have a lot of junk. My furniture is old, not worth much, so little by little their things replace mine. Of course, the house is mine, but I don't have much room in it now. But, what can I do, what can I say?

(Italian-Immigrant)

These limitations of personal space and decision-making are contributing factors to a gradual loss of the status and control which they once exercised. They now also have to adapt to a new living arrangement with their primary social supporters and identify the quality of interactions which would enhance their independence and well-being.

The central theme for these women focused on their need to maintain a sense of independence in their relationships with their primary social supporters. Reciprocity is the most significant issue for these aged Italian women. Their diminished physical health and income threaten to increase their dependence and reduce their capacity to reciprocate material and psychological support provided by their family members. This potential threat to the quality of their interpersonal transactions occurs at a time in their lifecycle when satisfying relationships are crucial for a sense of well-being.[25]

Maintaining independence presented an ongoing struggle and contradiction for these aged Italian women as they made certain adaptations in their daily lives to accommodate to the confines of their limited space and increasing physical vulnerability. Their struggle to maintain independence involved an ongoing dialectic between their need to depend on their primary supporters and their need not to become dependent on them. In other words, on account of their physical disability, these aged women have to live with their primary supporters for their daily needs to be met. However, in having these daily needs met, they also need to retain control of their own lives and continue to make choices for themselves. Issues of power and dependency became central in their daily lives—how to maintain a sense of power/control and purpose while still being dependent on others.

These women's struggle to maintain independence is greatly influenced by their gender, class, and ethnicity. These influences are evident in their self-image: how they perceived and described themselves; how they value themselves as women and as aged Italian women from a working-class background; and how they regard their personal resources, which they have invested throughout their lives in both work and family relationships. The resources which these aged women do or did possess refer to their education, financial situation, type of employment, and the available time which they have had for their children, for community activities, and/or leisure. The position of control established throughout their lives determines to a very large extent the resistances to dependence and constraints on independence they display in their advanced years.

The data of the present study support Leonard's argument that elderly people's struggle to maintain independence within their relationships is socially constructed so as to reflect the major social factors existing in our society.[26]

Within each social factor, Leonard contends that two groups exist with one at either end of the continuum. One group represents those who have more resources, better life chances and consequently, more power. The other group consists of those who have fewer resources, poorer life chances, and hence, less power. Being in control of their own lives as much as possible, and making choices for themselves necessarily implies that care-receivers continue to be in a position of power. In this study, the Italian-Canadian group of aged women fared as the group having more resources, better life chances (i.e. education, working conditions, financial stability), and hence more control; and the Italian-Immigrant group of women as the group having fewer resources, poorer life chances, and hence, less control over their experiences as care-receivers.

Highly relevant to these aged women's struggle to maintain independence or to resist dependence is the concept of reciprocity, which involves an exchange of a valued resource or service for a needed resource or service. Within any primary social support system, there are physical, emotional, economic and social resources that can be exchanged in a reciprocal manner, depending on the needs of the family members. It is a fact that as aged care-receivers, these women rely on the resources of their families; however, there is growing evidence to suggest that family members also turn to their aged parents for assistance during times of stress.[27]

Data from this study reveal significant contributions made to family resources by the Italian-Canadian group of women. These women acted as resources to their adult children by providing for specific instrumental and emotional needs. For instance, some of these women gave substantial amounts of money to help their children purchase a home or pay for bills due to unemployment or unexpected crises. Others were faced with adult children experiencing emotional problems most often associated with a marital problem, divorce, or major illness. These women generally saw their contribution as one of making themselves available when their child needed to talk or needed help, but avoiding offering unsolicited advice. This pattern is directly related to the interactions they engaged in during earlier years. Because these women had more time, they were often available for their children. Consequently, this accessibility developed into a resource which they were able to use in exchange for support.

> Two of my sons divorced. It involved six children in all. It was a mess. They told me it was their affair, so I didn't pry. My concern was for the children. I took care of the grandchildren.
>
> (Italian-Canadian)

> I was afraid to live in my big house alone. So, I sold it and moved to live on the top flat of my daughter's duplex. But, then this daughter separated and divorced her husband and she moved to another place. So, I moved in with her and paid a portion of the rent and other expenses.
>
> (Italian-Canadian)

This balance in the exchange of resources enables these women to resist dependence. They are in a position that enables them to resist dependence through private negotiations with their primary social supporters.

However, when aged women have nothing valuable to give in return for the tangible and intangible goods and services they receive from their primary social supporters, their independence is jeopardized and they become dependent. Due to their lack of resources, they feel indebted and that they are taking disproportionately more than they are giving in return. Hence, they perceive themselves to be in a subordinate or dependent position relative to their caregivers. The following statements reflect mainly the perceptions of aged Italian-Immigrant women.

> It was fine when I helped out with their children, the cooking, and the cleaning. Now, that I need help, the rules have changed. I have nothing of value to offer them any more. So I resign myself. I live in this room. If they visit, fine. If they ask me to join them, fine. If not, then I'm alone. They want their freedom. They don't want me to meddle ... I've learned to accept it, to do the best I can.
>
> (Italian-Immigrant)

> When you are old and no good like myself, your children do you a favour in looking after you ... Old age is hard. You're not good for anything.

You can't do what you used to do. My son and
his family are too helpful … I can't do anything
for them.

(Italian-Immigrant)

As care-receivers, these women find themselves lacking in
valuable resources since they are no longer able to provide for
the instrumental needs of their families. Throughout their
lives, these women worked, struggled, and sacrificed for their
families. Their domestic and paid work focused mostly on the
instrumental tasks needed in settling in and establishing their
families in a new homeland. This process placed tremendous
constraints on their time. Findings show that time constraints
meant less time to respond to emotional needs of family members. Consequently, this lack of past resources, along with
strong feelings of current indebtedness place these women in
a dependent position vis-à-vis their primary social supporters.
Constraints on their independence were most evident in their
inability to negotiate. Since they felt they had no assets, they
were not in any position to negotiate for specific needs.
Hence, they remained silent and felt dependent as care-
receivers.

Even though studies consistently argue that family members do accept the responsibility of providing help to an aged
relative in need and that they do so for a variety of reasons
involving bonds of affection and/or feelings of obligation, an
increasing number of these studies[28] also document the stress
and strain of caregiving, and raise the issue of the influence
primary social supporters exert in encouraging their aged

relatives to maintain independence. The quality of the caring relationship is crucial because of its potential for promoting supportive alliances or non-supportive alliances for the care-receiver.

Supportive Alliances

Each caregiving relationship takes place within a personal historical context. Both the caregiver(s) and care-receiver enter the relationship with a history of particular interactions which may promote or impede future independence of the care-receiver. If the bonds of reciprocity and affection have been strong in the history of the relationship, they continue in the current relationship. According to the perception of these aged women, assistance or past services provided by the aged relative provide the basis for a continuing supportive alliance:

> I was there when they needed me. Now I need them and here they are.
>
> (Italian-Canadian)

> Now I reap the benefits. I sacrificed for them. My children, if I need whatever, they are always here. They give me lots of care.
>
> (Italian-Immigrant)

A history of supportive alliances encourages these Italian women to remain independent by promoting a process of interdependence. However, interdependence in these care-giving relationships is possible only if some type of resource is available. As discussed above, the aged Italian-Canadian group of women were found to have more resources, and consequently displayed a more successful resistance to dependence than did the aged Italian-Immigrant group of women. Similarly, the findings indicate that these same Italian-Canadian women have, through an exchange of resources, promoted more control in their lives and are now making more choices for themselves than do the Italian-Immigrant group. When Italian-Immigrant women have resources to share, they experience control and availability of options similar to the Italian-Canadian group. Sharing information, a co-operative approach to decision-making, and the provision of emotional and financial support are specific examples identified by these women as enhancing their independence.

> When my husband passed away, I stayed here alone for the second year, I told the children that I would have to sell the house. I can't live here, not because I'm scared … I can't take care of the house. My arthritis is very bad. So I said to my children, one of you has to come back or else I'll sell. None of the children answered me that night. Two or three days later, my daughter and her husband came by and said, "Don't sell the house, we'll come back." It was five years ago.
>
> (Italian-Canadian)

> My daughter is alone. Her husband has left her
> and the children ... We live together. She helps
> me but I also help her ... She talks to me about
> her problems ... I listen ... I encourage the
> children ... together we manage. With my pen-
> sion, I help to pay the bills.
>
> (Italian-Canadian)

These women perceive their primary social supporters as friends. They do not acknowledge that a role reversal or shift in responsibilities has occurred between themselves and their family member(s); rather, they perceive that an adaptation of roles and responsibilities has occurred in order to accommodate to changes in their everyday realities. The interdependence of interactions is crucial in understanding the quality of their relationships. In these cases, durability of the helping alliances stems from the practical and emotional functions that family members fulfil for the aged relative and, similarly, the input that the aged person has into the family.

Non-Supportive Alliances

Highly relevant to the quality of the social support of these aged care-receivers is the issue of interdependence, which we define here as an individual being able to give and receive resources. If an imbalance arises in the exchanges within the support system, the resulting tension may foster non-supportive exchanges between caregivers and care-receivers and, consequently, interfere with the promotion of independence. At the same time, the very stress of caregiving is frequently cited as affecting the quality of care given to aged relatives.[29] In some cases, the aged care-receiver is forced into a dependent position on account of the stress and strain experienced by the caregiver(s). Both Talbott and Matthews have addressed this issue of non-supportive alliances and the dependent role of aged care-receivers. Matthews' analysis of this power differential follows the argument that the older mother is less powerful in the family precisely because she is lacking resources, both financial and social, to exchange with her children; and often she does not have access to other relationships from which she can obtain what she needs. The findings of this study support that argument.

> My son and my daughter-in-law are fighting with each other. I know it's because of me ... I don't know what to do. I can't do anything ... I don't know what will happen.
>
> (Italian-Immigrant)

> I'm no longer in charge of anything. That's what hurts me the most! Especially since it is I who has worked the hardest in this family. However, if you talk to her (the daughter), she'll tell you all about her problems. She'll also tell you that I'm one of her biggest problems. In fact, she'll tell you that I'm the cause of all her stress. If you interview her, you'll find out how terrible I am.
>
> (Italian-Immigrant)

Gerontological studies and feminist research have under-scored the fact that women acting as primary social sup-porters may experience stress as they perform various services for their aged relatives. However, in recent years, research has increasingly focused on investigating the issue of abuse of aged care-receivers.[30] In the literature, elder abuse has come to be regarded by many as anything that threatens the well-being of an aged person. It encompasses several types of maltreatment: physical, psychological, financial, and neglect; and it can involve acts of commission or omission on the part of the caregiver, who is often a person the aged person loves and trusts. This present study supports the argument that non-supportive alliances between caregiver and care-receiver result from the stresses of the caring relationship and promote the dependence of the aged care-receiver.

Financial abuse, psychological abuse, and neglect were the main types of maltreatment described by these aged women. These types of abuses force care-receivers to withdraw into passivity. They are confined to an existence of dependence, from which it is difficult to extricate themselves. Their non-supportive alliances foster dependency in that they render these women helpless, subordinate, and voiceless in articulating their needs, and exclude them from decision-making regarding their own situations.

In summary, the findings indicate that the quality of the relationship between care-receiver and primary supporters depends on the quality of the previous relationship between the woman and her family members. If there has been an equitable exchange of resources, the data show that this exchange of resources will continue into the current caring relationship, allowing the care-receiver to negotiate reciprocity and achieve interdependence. This alliance is supportive. However, the alliance becomes non-supportive when the care-receiver lacks equitable resources to exchange. Then the care-receiver becomes dependent and is at risk of abuse.

Impact on Well-Being

How these women perceived whether they were encouraged or inhibited in their expression of giving, as well as receiving, had a direct impact on their well-being.

> I help with some of the cooking and cleaning. I take it slowly. I do what I can. It helps them a little because they are all working, but it helps me a lot … I feel useful.
>
> (Italian-Canadian)

> I do nothing. They do everything. They tell me that it is easier for them if they do it for me … I do nothing, they do everything. (cries)
>
> (Italian-Immigrant)

Studies have repeatedly shown that supportive relationships that are characterized by excessive receiving can be detrimental to an individual's well-being, in contrast to relationships that are reciprocal.[31] The aged women in this study have provided further support for this argument. As their power resources decline due to their chronic illness, the ability of these women to give as well as receive support becomes a major concern.

The findings have been interpreted to indicate the struggles these aged women experience in maintaining their independence, influenced both by the structural factors of their gender, class, and ethnicity and by the quality of the relationship with their primary social supporters. The group of aged Italian-Canadian women displayed more resistance to dependence because of their better life chances and the greater resources they had experienced throughout their lives. As a result, many of these women had been able to develop and maintain alliances with their primary social supporters, and also to maintain some control over their lives; whereas the group of aged Italian-Immigrant women described many more constraints on their independence due to their poor life chances and limited resources. Many of these women now find themselves dependent on their primary social supporters and lacking control over their situations.

These women's perceptions of being or not being in control of their present situations have a tremendous impact on their well-being. The two main indicators of well-being used in the study were self-esteem and life satisfaction.[32] These women were asked questions regarding their beliefs about their self-worth, their ability to think well of themselves and their appraisal of both their past and present lives. The following paragraphs highlight the positive impact that results from feelings of being in control, in contrast to the negative impact associated with feelings of powerlessness.

Positive Impact

Self-determination refers to a person's ability to control their lives and to make choices.[33] Individuals in this position are more likely to think well of themselves and perceive their lives as being more satisfying. Those aged women who perceived themselves as being in control of their care-receiving situations were actively involved in their own decisions and were able to live a life of their own choosing. The following statements illustrate the diversity of responses regarding their perception of control in their current situations.

> I don't want to sell the house right now. When I'm ready to sell the house, I will inform the children. I am very independent. This is my house. I organize the kind of help I need. I tell my children what they can help me with.
>
> (Italian-Canadian)

> I still make the decisions … I'm adapting as I go along. I'm expecting to go. We are all going. I'm no different. I just want to finish tidying up all my affairs before going. I have already organized my burial plot.
>
> (Italian-Canadian)

> I am receiving pension money. I am in charge of my affairs. I don't owe my children anything. I decide what I need. I pay for everything I need.
>
> (Italian-Immigrant)

I need my own place, even if it means moving into a nursing facility. I have already looked into the matter, and have initiated the process of moving in ... I know what a burden an old sick person imposes on the family. I don't want my family to feel like that about me. We agreed, my children and I, that I will be moving into a nursing facility. They have their responsibilities towards their families. And, I want to remain independent as much as possible from them. I don't mind being dependent on strangers, but I don't want to be on my children; to be a burden on them — no, never.

(Italian-Canadian)

These women were able to define their needs, to influence and effect change so as to have their needs acknowledged or fulfilled in collaboration with their primary social supporters. Hence, these women expressed positive statements about their self-worth, looked forward with interest to their future, and looked back on their own life histories with satisfaction. They did not see their lives as totally successful but they did not express regret, wishing that things had been different.

I've lived a good life ... I've always been healthy ... What do you expect at my age? ... Life continues to change. I have no choice, my friends passed away, my husband also. So I have to adjust and accept. My children, grandchildren, and great-grandchildren, they make me what I am. They make me proud, so I deal with life the best way I can.

(Italian-Canadian)

I don't plan too much ahead. I'm too sick to do that. It just comes as it goes, and unless something's going on or I'm going somewhere, or we're going to do something, then okay. If something comes up, if I like it, I say okay. But apart from that, I take one day at a time. I'm happy the way I am, I have a good life.

(Italian-Canadian)

I like to go out, that's all ... I know I'm going to die but not right away, so there's plenty for me to do and see. I take care of myself. There are times I'm sick, very sick, and I need care, but there are other times I like to go out. That's my future plans ... I expect to die, but to live a good life till then.

(Italian-Canadian)

Briefly, these aged women have emphasized that their interdependence with their helping alliances permits them to have some self-determination without the rigours of total independence. Hence, the distinguishing features of these women include their positive self-assessment of their worth and life satisfaction. The following section, however, contrasts positive impact on well-being with the everyday reality of those aged women who feel the loss of control and feel dependent on their primary social supports.

Negative Impact

Loss of control that results directly from the tension that exists between care-receivers and their primary social supporters, and the heightened influences resulting from their gender, class, and ethnicity lead to feelings of powerlessness. These aged Italian women have expressed these feelings of perceived powerlessness in relation to their primary social supporters. Studies have defined powerlessness as a perceived lack of personal control of events in the care-receiving situation. A typical comment stated by an aged woman is:

> I'm no longer in charge of what goes on in my home. The decisions are made by my family because they have to fit into their schedule. I just listen and agree. I'm back to being a little girl. What they say, I do. I don't have a choice. I'm not in control.
>
> (Italian-Immigrant)

It is very clear from these data that these feelings have a devastating effect on the well-being of these women. They have a limited amount of energy available to deal with constraints on their independence and consequently see no value in themselves and no reason to expect things to improve or even to wish that circumstances would improve. The aged woman either envisions having no future or sees a radically altered future. She may also believe that because of her chronic illness all control over her future has been lost.

> They used to depend on me. Now, I'm dependent on them. I'm not happy to be under their control (cries). I constantly think of dying. Each day, I could get another paralysis and it could be the end.
>
> (Italian-Immigrant)

> I am nothing. I cannot do anything, any more ... My husband has to do everything for me, or my son. So, I find myself too discouraged. What I was able to do, now I can't ... Do you understand? This is my life. It's very sad. It's a tragedy!
>
> (Italian-Immigrant)

> Nothing. There is nothing in my life ... Not worth even thinking about it. This is the way of life now.
>
> (Italian-Immigrant)

In the everyday experience of these aged women, their feelings of powerlessness have manifested themselves in the form of depression and loneliness.

Summary and Conclusion

The experiences of aged Italian women have been described. Their experiences highlight their departure from dependent roles, growth in their autonomy and status, their encounters with chronic illness, and their consequently changed statuses. These women have disclosed their vulnerabilities, as well as their strengths in their everyday lives. The impact of chronic illness has been a tremendous challenge to their self-image and consequent well-being.

In contrast to previous research which supports the assumption that care-receivers react positively to the care given to them by their primary social supporters, the findings reported in this study show that care-receivers react along a positive and negative continuum depending on the quality of the caring relationship. The crucial aspect determining the quality of the relationship rests on the care-receiver's struggle to maintain control over her life. This struggle to maintain independence is affected by certain interrelated influences of the care-receivers' gender, class, and ethnicity. These influences, then, have an impact on the quality of the caring relationship, determining whether the alliances will be either supportive by enhancing interdependence between the care-receiver and caregiver, or non-supportive by encouraging dependence of the care-receiver on the caregiver.

The findings further indicate that the Italian-Canadian group of aged women were more in control in the exchange of resources, achieving reciprocity, and negotiating interdependence with their primary supporters than were the

Italian-Immigrant group. Since the Italian-Canadian women had better life chances because of their education, employment, and financial situations, these women had more time to invest in developing relationships with their children in which exchanges transpired and which established the groundwork for the eventual caring relationship between the care-receiver and caregiver(s). In contrast, the Italian-Immigrant group of women experienced poorer life chances and had greater constraints on their time, due to their ever-present need to earn enough money to survive and to establish their families in a new homeland. As a result, the findings suggest that the aged Italian-Canadian group of women have established more interdependence with their supporters, which reflects the supportive aspects of their alliances, while the aged Italian-Immigrant group of women are more dependent on their primary supporters, which reflects a non-supportive aspect to the caring relationships.

The intra-ethnic differences that exist between these women should be used to provide insight into the abilities they developed over their lifespans to deal with the constraints imposed on them by social structures. This redefinition of the disadvantages experienced by these women involves removing the causes of the oppression from the individual and placing them on the social context of the individual's life; this has the effect of empowering the person and enhancing self-esteem. This focus encompasses and has implications for the social and psychological well-being of the care-receiver. The challenge posed by these findings is how to provide services which will encourage care-receivers to remain in control and to make decisions for themselves so as to improve the quality of their lives.

Notes

1. Marshall 1987.
2. Qureshi and Walker 1989.
3. Treas and Bengston 1987; Wigdor and Fletcher 1990.
4. Aronson 1988, 1990; Evers 1984, 1985.
5. Association Québécoise de Gérontologie 1989; Dallaire and Martin 1989.
6. Dallaire and Martin 1989.
7. Driedger and Chappell 1987.
8. Baker 1988; MacLean, Siew, Fowler and Graham 1987.
9. Lowenstein 1983; Nomme Russell 1989.
10. Gambino 1974.
11. Cowell 1986; Johnson 1985; Smith 1978.
12. Cowell 1986; Johnson 1985.
13. Bernard 1975.
14. Iacovetta 1986a, 1986b.
15. Boyd 1986; Miedema and Nason-Clark 1989; Simon and Brettell 1986.
16. Cellini 1978; Denis 1986.
17. Simon and Brettell 1986.
18. Boyd 1986; Simon and Brettell 1986.
19. Simon and Brettell 1986.
20. Belgrave 1986; Corbin and Strauss 1988; Hooyman and Kiyak 1991.
21. Horowitz, Silverstone and Reinhardt 1991; Talbott 1990.
22. Cantor and Little 1985; Noelker and Poulshock 1982; Talbott 1990.
23. Noelker and Poulshock 1982.
24. Talbott 1990.
25. Rook 1987.
26. Leonard 1987.
27. Greenberg and Becker 1988.
28. Miller, McFall and Montgomery 1991; Quinn-Musgrove 1990
29. Long 1991.
30. McDonald, Hornick, Robertson and Wallace 1991; Pillemer and Wolf 1986.
31. Antonucci and Akiyamma 1987; Ingersoll-Dayton and Antonucci 1988; Rook 1987.
32. Thomas 1988.
33. Weick and Pope 1988.

References

Antonucci, T., and Akiyamma, H. (1987). "Social networks in adult life and a preliminary examination of the convoy model." *Journal of Gerontology,* 42(5), 519-527.

Aronson, J. (1988). *Women's experiences in giving and receiving care: Pathways to social change.* Unpublished doctorate thesis, University of Toronto.

Aronson, J. (1990). "Old women's experiences of needing care: Choice or compulsion." *Canadian Journal of Aging,* 9(3), 234-247.

Association Québécoise De Gérontologie. (1989). "Vieillir au féminin." *Le Gérontophile: Revue trimestrielle de l'association québécoise de gérontologie,* Montréal, Université du Québec, 11(1), 1-271.

Baker, M. (1988). *Aging in a Canadian Society.* Montréal: McGraw-Hill Ryerson Ltd.

Belgrave, L.L. (1986). *The experience of chronic disease in the everyday lives of elderly women.* Doctorate thesis, Cleveland, OH: Case Western Reserve University.

Bernard, J. (1975). *Women, Wives, Mothers: Values and Options.* Chicago: Aldine Publishing Co.

Boyd, M. (1986). "Immigrant women in Canada." In R.J. Simon and C.B. Cretell (eds.), *International Migration: The Female Experience* (pp. 45-61). NJ: Rowman and Allanheld.

Cantor, M., and Little, V. (1985). "Aging and social care." In R. Binstock and E. Shanas (eds.), *Handbook of Aging and the Social Sciences* (pp. 745-781). New York: Van Nostrand Reinhold.

Cellini, L. (1978). "Emigration, the Italian family, and changing roles." In B.B. Caroli, R.F. Harney, and L.F. Tomasi (eds.), *The Italian Immigrant Woman in North America.* Toronto: The Multicultural History Society of Ontario.

Corbin, J.M., and Strauss, A. (1988). *Unending Work and Care: Managing Chronic Illness at Home.* London: Jossey-Bass Publishers.

Cowell, D.D. (1986). "Growing up and growing old in Italian-American families by C.L. Johnson." *The International Journal on Aging* 23(12), 129-130.

Dallaire, H., and Martin, E. (1989). "Solitude et dépendance: La situation de la femme agée." *Le Gérontophile,* 11(1), 8-11.

Denis, A.B. (1986). "Adaptation to multiple subordination? Women in vertical mosaic." *Canadian Ethnic Studies,* XVIII(3), 61-74.

Dreidger, L., and Chappell, N. (1987). *Aging and Ethnicity: Toward an Interface.* Toronto: Butterworths.

Evers, H. (1984). "Old women's self-perceptions of dependency and some important implications for service provision." *Journal of Epidemiology and Community Health,* 38(4), 306-309.

_____ (1985). "The frail elderly woman: Emergent questions in aging and women's health." In E. Lewin and V. Olesen (eds.). *Women, Health and Healing: Toward a New Perspective,* (pp. 86-112). New York: Tavistock Publication.

Gambino, R. (1974). *Blood of My Blood: The Dilemma of the Italian-Americans.* New York: The Free Press.

Greenberg, J.S., and Becker, M. (1988). "Aging parents as family resources." *The Gerontologist,* 28(6), 786-791.

Hooyman, N., and Kiyak, A. (1991). *Social Gerontology.* MA: Allyn and Bacon.

Horowitz, A., Silverstone, B.M., and Reinhardt, J.P. (1991). "A conceptual and empirical exploration of personal autonomy issues within family caregiving relationships." *The Gerontologist,* 31(1), 23-31.

Iacovetta, F. (1986a). "From 'Contadina' to worker: Southern Italian immigrant working women in Toronto, 1947-1962." In J. Burnet (ed.), *Looking into My Sister's Eyes: An Exploration in Women's History* (pp. 195-222). Toronto: The Multicultural History Society of Ontario.

_____ (1986b). "Southern Italian working women." *Polyphony,* 8(1/2), 56-60.

Ingersoll-Dayton, B., and Antonucci, T. (1988). "Reciprocal and nonreciprocal social support: Contrasting sides of intimate relationships." *Journal of Gerontology,* 43(3), pp. 565-573.

Johnson, C.L. (1985). *Growing Up and Growing Old in Italian-American Families.* New Jersey: Rutgers University Press.

Leonard, P. (1987). "Dependency, gender and class in old age." In Paper presented at the 55th Congress of the Association Canadienne-Française pour l'Avancement des Sciences, Université d'Ottawa, May.

Long, C.M. (1991). "Family care of the elderly: Stress, appraisal, and coping." *Journal of Applied Gerontology,* 19(3), 311-327.

Lowenstein, S.F. (1983). "A feminist perspective." In A. Rosenblatt and D. Waldfogel (eds.), *Handbook of Clinical Social Work,* (pp. 518-543). San Francisco: Jossey-Bass.

MacLean, M.J., Siew, N. Fowler, D. and Graham, I. (1987). "Institutional racism in old age: Theoretical perspectives and a case study about access to social services." *Canadian Journal on Aging,* 6(2), 128-140.

Marshall, V. (1987). "Social perspectives on aging." In V. Marshall (ed.), *Aging in Canada: Social perspectives* (2nd ed.) (pp. 1-8). Toronto: Fitzhenry and Whiteside.

Matthews, S.H. (1979). *The Social World of Women.* London: Sage Publications.

McDonald, P.L., Hornick, J.P., Robertson, G.B., and Wallace, J.E. (1991). *Elder Abuse and Neglect in Canada.* Toronto: Butterworths.

Miedema, B., and Nason-Clark, N. (1989). "Second class status: An analysis of the lived experiences of immigrant women in Fredericton." *Canadian Ethnic Studies,* XXI(2), 61-73.

Miller, B., McFall, S., and Montgomery, A. (1991). "The impact of elder health, caregiver involvement, and global stress on two dimensions of caregiver burden." *Journal of Gerontology: Social Sciences* 46(1), 59-519.

Noelker, L.S., and Poulshock, S.W. (1982). *The Effects on Families of Caring For Impaired Elderly in Residence.* Final report submitted to the Administration on Aging. Cleveland, OH: The Margaret Blenkner Research Centre for Family Studies, The Benjamin Rose Institute.

Nomme Russell, M. (1989). "Feminist social work skills." *Canadian Social Work Review* 6(1), 69-81.

Pillemer, K., and Wolf, R. (eds.). (1986). *Elder Abuse: Conflict in the Family.* Dover, MA: Auburn House Publishing, Co.

Quereshi, H., and Walker, A. (1989). *The Caring Relationship: Elderly People and Their Families.* London: Macmillan.

Quinn-Musgrove, S.L. (1990). "Extended care-giving: The experience of surviving spouses." *Journal of Women and Aging,* 2(2), 93-107.

Rochon, J. (1987). *Commission d'Enquête sur les Services de Santé et les Services Sociaux.* Québec: Ministère des Affaires Sociales.

Rook, K.S. (1987). "Reciprocity of social exchange and social satisfaction among older women." *Journal of Personality and Social Psychology,* 52(1), 145-154.

Simon, R.J., and Brettell, C.B. (1986). "Immigrant women: An introduction." In R.J. Simon and C.B. Brettell (eds.), *International Migration: The Female Experience* (pp. 3-19). NJ: Rowman and Allanheld.

Smith, J.E. (1978). "Italian mothers, American daughters; Changes in work and family roles." In B.B. Caroli, R.F. Harney and L.F. Tomasi (eds.), *The Italian Immigrant Woman in North America* (pp. 206-221). Toronto: The Multicultural History Society of Ontario.

Talbott, M.M. (1990). "The negative side of the relationship between older widows and their adult children: The mother's perspective." *The Gerontologist,* 30(5), 595-603.

Thomas, B. (1988). "Self-esteem and life satisfaction." *Journal of Gerontological Nursing,* 14, 25-29.

Treas, J., and Bengston, V.L. (1987). "The family in later years." In M.B. Sussman and S.K. Steinmetz (eds.), *Handbook of Marriage and the Family* (pp. 625-648). New York: Plenum Press.

Weick, A., and Pope, L. (1988). "Knowing what's best: A new look at self-determination." *The Journal of Contemporary Social Work*, (1), 10-16.

Wigdor, B.T., and Fletcher, S. (1990). *NACA Position on Informal Caregiving: Support and Enhancement*. Ontario: The National Advisory Council on Aging.

4

Health Realities and Independence: The Voice of Elderly Women

Michael J. MacLean, Nancy Houlahan, Frances B. Barskey

Introduction

As the phenomenon of individual and population aging becomes a significant social issue in the latter part of the twentieth century, there is an increasing interest in understanding how elderly people in Western societies can maintain independence, despite an inevitable decline in their physical health. Elderly people themselves are very concerned with maintaining their physical and mental health as much as possible, and they are determined to meet the challenges to their autonomy.[1] Family caregivers, social workers, health care practitioners and researchers are equally interested in providing for the health of elderly people and devote much energy to ensuring that they have the physical and mental resources to maintain their independence for as long as possible.[2] Furthermore, social policy analysts within government organizations and in other provincial and federal institutions are concerned with promoting policies related to the improvement of health and independence of seniors: the Seniors' Independence Program, the Seniors' Independence Research Program and the Health Promotion Unit within Canada Health and Welfare are examples of only three programmes in this area.

There are both social and personal reasons to be concerned about the health and independence of elderly people. One social reason is that Western societies place great emphasis on individual initiative and independence throughout the life cycle. This emphasis encourages children, young adults, middle-aged adults and seniors to accept a narrow definition of both independence and dependence, a definition that suggests that independence involves characteristics such as strength, forcefulness, leadership, power, and autonomy, whereas dependence is characterized by terms such as weakness, following, powerlessness, and burden. Dominant discourse sees both independence and dependence as individual characteristics rather than as a dynamic interpersonal process. Dependence is tolerated—but certainly not encouraged—in childhood, but for all other age groups, the message is clear: independence is the socially-accepted goal.

Another reason for concern is that health and independence have been inextricably linked, since good health is seen as being related to independence and poor health to dependence: the contrast is between a healthy productive unit and an unhealthy "burden on the economy." As has been clearly documented in many health and aging studies, which invariably use a narrower definition of physical health rather than functional health, there is a strong and indisputable link between aging and declining health.[3] These findings convincingly show that the majority of elderly people are in poorer health than when they were younger; but because they rely on that narrower definition of physical health they lead to the conservative conclusion that most elderly people are also dependent.

In addition to these social reasons for interest in the relationship between health and independence in an increasingly aging population, there are also individual and material reasons specific to the groups who are involved in the dynamics of individual and population aging. Elderly people, for example, are clearly interested in maintaining their health and independence in later life, since a lack of these qualities means a lack of options for exercising control. Most seniors have exercised considerable control over their adult lives and are not disposed to giving it up simply because they have reached an arbitrary age or because their health is deteriorating. Seniors are also very aware of the limited options available to them should their health and independence decline: to be cared for by their family (if available) or in institutions. The family option is often hard to accept because seniors may see themselves as contributing to double dependence; the dependence of the senior, and the reduction in the caregiving family's independence because of the resources devoted to the care of the elderly person. This appears to lead an elderly person to develop a perception of self as a "burden" on the family, a perception fostered by a society that strongly favours those who produce in an economic sense. It is safe to say that most people, of any age, would hesitate to enter a relationship in which they were associated with being a "burden," so that the family care option is fraught with stress and contradiction. The institutional option is also difficult to accept because of the unappealing scenario it usually entails. It often means going into a large long-term care institution, a form of living different from any other that most seniors have previously experienced. It is also an option that requires the senior to give up a great deal of independence, and hand over control of many aspects of her life to strangers on a long-term basis.

Health and independence are special concerns for elderly women. For married women (the vast majority of women in the present over-sixty-five age cohort are, or have been, married)[4] it is well-known that they are usually younger than their husbands, live longer than their husbands, and that their marriage rate after bereavement is lower than that of widowers, leaving many older women with decreased social support.[5] In fact, it has been argued convincingly that widowhood is an expected life event for women, and that women who have married can expect to spend a significant number of years as widows.[6] As these widows have spent their lives in a patriarchical society, they have been seen, in the traditional sense, as having been dependent on their husbands. However, the social issue of dependency is much more complex.[7] It can be expected that these widows had striven for a considerable amount of independence throughout their lives, and would continue to strive to maintain it in their later years. On the other hand, it is well-documented that, for structural reasons, elderly women are poorer than men and may find it increasingly difficult to manage financially in old age.[8] For women who have been unmarried throughout their lives, issues of health and independence are also important because of the social and psychological experiences they have had of living in a society where familial patriarchal ideology has played a central role in defining women. From this brief analysis, it can be argued that the social, individual and economic issues that all women face in later life have a significant impact on both their health and independence.

The concept of health is usually understood as multidimensional: it has been defined by policy makers as a "state of complete physical, mental and social well-being,"[9] and not merely the absence of disease or infirmity. This definition, similar to that given by the World Health Organization, is positive in that it incorporates physical, mental and social components of health rather than focusing on the narrow view that relates health only to physical issues. However, this definition seems to be based on an unrealistic expectation that people can experience a state of "complete physical, mental and social well-being" as well as the absence of disease and infirmity. It is not clear how this state can be achieved in any part of the lifecycle, and it is certainly doubtful that this state of health could be achieved by elderly people. It is a definition of health based, despite its reference to mental and social aspects of well-being, on a medical model that focuses on a cure for whatever is missing from this complete state of well-being.

Given such a definition of health, one which seems virtually unattainable, it is not surprising that research on health reveals considerable levels of illness. With respect to elderly women, research findings suggest that physical health is the single most important contributor to the quality of their lives.[10] Clearly, mental health also has a major impact on the general well-being and independence of elderly women. This point becomes particularly important when we consider that there are nearly twice as many women as men in all ages who are said to suffer from depression,[11] as measured by quantitative statistics related to the use of anti-depressive medicines, therapies and visits to mental health practitioners. Another factor that influences older women's health are their social support networks,[12] which consist of interaction with friends, neighbours, relatives, and community organizations. The loss of an important relationship with a spouse can decrease health resources and become a major concern for elderly widows.[13] However, the continuation of close ties with relatives, friends, and other forms of social support among elderly people acts as a buffer to stressful events, facilitates adjustments to losses that frequently accompany old age, and increases general well-being.[14] Thus, it is clear that health is an important and complex issue for elderly women, and it is not surprising that they devote considerable energy to maintaining good health in later life.

The concept of independence is also multi-dimensional and complex. For elderly people, independence in its most basic sense can be viewed as having some control over their lives, needs, and self-esteem.[15] In a broader sense, independence can be viewed in terms of personality, interpersonal relationships, or actions.[16] As health deteriorates, many elderly women may be forced to depend on others for care. The loss of a spouse in conjunction with declining health can affect an elderly woman's independence when her social support is reduced, and she may find that as a widow she is more dependent on others than she wants to be. On the other hand, Martin-Matthews suggests that after the initial psychological and social disruption of bereavement, many elderly women experience widowhood as an opportunity for growth and independence.[17] This is probably most true for widows who have adequate health and financial resources. The ability to remain self-supporting in their own homes is also an important consideration for elderly women. Lowy discusses how North American culture equates independence with strength, and dependence with weakness and personal deficit.[18] For healthy elderly women, the ability to continue to have control over their lives, to preserve their power and self-esteem, and to have continuity in their lives is of utmost importance.

This introduction has tried to establish that much research on the topic of women and aging stresses the importance of health and independence. However, the majority of this research is of a quantitative nature undertaken by younger male and female researchers and policy analysts about an issue that does not yet affect them directly. This is not to say that this research is not valuable; in fact, it is critical for research on aging to be developed by younger people, as well as by seniors, in order not to ghettoize the important issues that elderly people face. Structural issues related to class, gender, race, sexual orientation, disability and age, among others, are not issues which should be addressed only by those who are most affected. These structural issues affect everyone (although certainly some people more than others) and therefore everyone has a right to challenge them. However, it is always important to go to the source of information when one wants to consider an issue, and an increasing number of qualitative and feminist researchers are seeking out the views of elderly people on issues that have a significant impact on their lives.[19] Therefore, in the interest of contributing to knowledge on this topic through a qualitative and feminist approach, we feel it is important to obtain the views of healthy independent elderly women on these issues.

Connecting with the Voice of Women

This essay is based on a qualitative study that explores independent, healthy, elderly women's experiences of aging. To locate women whom we would expect would perceive themselves as both healthy and independent, we approached a women's social action group in Montréal called the Voice of Women (VOW). The Voice of Women is an international women's peace group which began in Canada in 1960. The group formed when women across the country wanted to speak out against the threat of nuclear war. It is the longest-standing women's peace group in Canada. The Voice of Women works for nuclear disarmament, human rights, justice, and other issues that affect women; it works especially against war or the threat of war as a method of exercising power. The Montréal VOW meets twice a month and holds three public meetings per year. There are currently eighty members in the VOW, of which sixteen are sixty-five years and older; these sixteen are among the most active of the eighty members.

We chose to study a social action group for women which, by its very nature, attracts women who are politically, environmentally, and socially aware. We chose the VOW instead of another of the many social action groups in which elderly women are involved such as Ploughshares, the National Advisory Council on the Status of Women, One Voice, Canadian Seniors for Social Responsibility, Amnesty International, or Pensioners for Peace, because Frances Barskey, one of the joint authors of this essay, is a long-time member of the VOW, and was able to make a significant link with other older women in this organization. To be involved with a social action group requires a personality that has definite views about issues, seeks out social change, and is willing to struggle for this change. Thus, in part because of their involvement with the VOW, we expected the women we interviewed to perceive themselves as being independent and healthy.

We made contact with a woman on the VOW membership committee who gave us the names of the sixteen members who were sixty-five years and older. We telephoned them and set up interviews with ten women who were willing to be interviewed. Of the ten women, eight were seventy-five years old or older while two were between the ages of sixty-five and seventy-four years old. All were white, middle-class women; all but one had worked outside of the home most of their lives; six were widowed, two never married, one separated, and one woman was married. From this brief description, it is evident that they are a select group in terms of their past working status outside the home, their long-time membership in the VOW, and the fact that they are middle-class. On the other hand, eight of these women were, or had been married, six were widowed, all saw themselves as independent and all had experienced age-related health problems. Given these characteristics, we felt that these women could give us some insights into issues of aging, health and independence which, to our knowledge, have not been documented elsewhere.

All ten women were interviewed in their own homes in the Montréal area. The interviews focused on: 1) key aspects of each woman's biography, family, and work history; 2) how she viewed her health and the health problems she encountered as she aged; 3) her thoughts on the issue of independence, including how she defined and maintained her own independence; and 4) her involvement with the Voice of Women. We explored connections between each woman's health and independence, and her involvement with the Voice of Women. Many themes about health and independence in the women's lives emerged from the interviews. For the purpose of this essay, however, the two main themes that emerged from the interviews may be summarized as functional health in later life, and independence as a life-long commitment.

Functional Health in Later Life

When discussing the topic of health with these women, many issues emerged, such as their own health, the health of their spouse or friends, and mental health in elderly females in general. Several women had had health problems which limited their activities in some way. None of them, however, was restricted from living in her own home as a result of health problems, and none needed major homecare support services. This fact attests to the individual strength of mind and independence of these women and the social advantages they have as a result of being in an economically independent position. The women have noticed their health slowly decline as they age and it frustrates them at times. A seventy-nine year old widow spoke of this realization:

> There isn't any question that the thing that strikes you most forcibly and tells you that you are a senior citizen, whether you want to believe it or don't, is declining health. It somehow seems to catch up with you.

While the women were frustrated and occasionally worried about their health, they did not perceive their problems as a threat to their independence. They dealt with the limitations they experienced in individual ways, but the general approach they tended to take was to focus on what they could do rather than what they could not do. This did not mean that they did not notice the losses they had experienced over the years. They certainly noticed that they could not do some activities as well as they had been able to in the past, but they kept coming back to what they could still do. In effect, they were talking about the reality of their functional health rather than an abstract view of unlimited or total health.

One major theme was how having outside interests helped the women maintain both health and independence as well as keeping them from worrying about their health. An example of this is given by a woman who, objectively, has experienced a major social loss (becoming a widow) and a major physical loss (loss of sight in one eye)—which may not be unusual for women of her age. This eighty year old widow belongs to a Yiddish group at the Golden Age Association (GAA). She worked as a seamstress her entire life and one project she does for the GAA is to make aprons for a craft sale. She stated:

> If I don't feel good, if the weather is no good, I
> say to myself, "So what. I have work to do." So I
> sit down at the machine and I work.

She also takes great pride in her accomplishments and what she is able to do:

> It helps me go on living, because I like it (making
> aprons), you see. You make one and you look at
> it and you say, "I made it. It looks so beautiful."

Her partial vision does not deter her from keeping active even though she stated that she does not do as much as she did in the past. Again, in what she says, it is clear that she is focusing on her functional health rather than on an abstract view of health:

> I say I'll do as much as I can. I'll do as much as I can and I am not going to blame it (the loss of one eye) on you or on somebody else.

It is evident that this woman has made a significant adjustment to a major physical loss. However, this kind of adjustment was a recurring theme emerging from the interviews with each of these women. We were struck by the equanimity with which they dealt with losses that appear psychologically and physically devastating. For example, another woman who is eighty years old and widowed, stated that she has weak bladder muscles that awaken her often in the night. It would be expected that this would be a major concern for her (and, indeed, given that she mentioned it, we assume that it has some implications for her), as it means a constant disruption of sleep and anxiety about incontinence. However, when asked about her personal health she replied by telling us about her recent literary activities. She began writing short stories two years ago at age seventy-eight. The stories are recollections and reminiscences of her childhood and have been published in Canada and the United States in both English and Yiddish journals. She is very proud of this accomplishment and stated that she receives great pleasure from it. In answering a direct question about her health, she said:

> I have the usual aches and pains, you know, but as soon as an idea comes into my head the aches and pains vanish and the writing begins ... What I feel about old age is that it is what you make of it. Of course, old age can be wearisome ... you know, most people are bound not to feel well. But when you have an absorbing interest like I have now in the writing ... and when they send me the articles ... and you get the letter from Toronto asking your permission to include it in an anthology, you say, "Boy, I've never had it so good."

A main interest that these women shared, and which they indicated had an important impact on their present attitudes toward their physical and mental health, was their involvement with the VOW. Involvement with the group differed for each woman but all had been longtime members with a strong commitment to the organization. Even the women who were not as active as they previously had been stated that they support the organization, pay their membership fees, receive literature and telephone calls about upcoming events and continue to feel that they are in touch with the VOW. An eighty-one year old single woman summed up this view by stating that she could no longer make it to the meetings.

... but I certainly believe in the VOW as an organization. I believe in what they stand for.

Another woman, a seventy-eight year old widow, stressed how important it was for her to continue to belong to the VOW:

> It keeps you more active. You keep in touch with people ... with events ... with people that you have known a good long time. You feel comfortable ... It is very important.

Two other women stated that the political involvement related to membership in the VOW was very important to their perception of their health. A seventy-nine year old widow summed up her involvement with the VOW and its relation to her health in the following manner:

> Well, I am convinced that thinking about other peoples' problems is great therapy as compared with stressing your own needs and wallowing in self-pity. And you can always wallow in self-pity because you are a widow, and you are alone,... and there is nobody here, and your children are away .... But you know, you don't have time if you realize that there are people who are in prison because they were unjustly convicted .... If you think that there are seniors, senior women particularly, who are impoverished without any

aid at all. If you think of drug addicts .... If you consider all these social problems that need recognition you don't have time to worry about your own health problems.

And another woman who was seventy-one years and separated stated:

And if you are with people who are active and whose mind is functioning all the time, it helps you. And in terms of your physical being, I mean if you are healthy mentally, you are much more likely to be healthy physically.

These quotes reflect a sense of the importance that these women place on being a member of the VOW. It appears that the social support provided by the VOW contributes to the women's general health and well-being. This is despite the fact that most of the women stated that they were not as active now in the organization as they had been in the past. This sentiment again seems to be illustrating the concept of functional health that is a recurring theme in the comments made regarding their self-perceptions of health. That is, they seem to be saying, in a positive way, that they consider many aspects of their lives in a functional sense—so that they think about what they can do rather than about what they cannot do. However, it also seems to be their main defining principle with respect to their social activism: they acknowledge that they are not as active in the VOW as they used to be, but it is still important to do what they can since these activities added significance to their lives, increased their self-esteem, kept them busy, kept them in touch with friends, and gave them a cause to fight for.

Each woman had at least one health problem which frustrated her at times and some of the women would be considered to have major health problems. However, each used interests such as dancing, sewing, writing, socializing and involvement with the VOW as ways of getting over specific health problems and getting on with other aspects of their life. The women found that keeping a focus on areas of interest helped them maintain their physical and mental health as it kept both their minds and bodies active.

This does not mean that they minimized the health losses they have experienced, but simply that they make use of the health resources that they still have. This functional approach to physical health is also carried over to their social commitment through the VOW, where they continue to be as involved as their resources allow. The message here is that, despite a natural decline in resources, one can still function as an active member of an organization to which one has a commitment. Although the level of functioning may be less than it was before, that does not necessarily mean that the level of commitment is any less. This functional health statement is a positive and realistic message from these women because it challenges us to do what we can with what we have, rather than being preoccupied with what we have lost. That this is very healthy is reflected by one of the women we interviewed:

And you do as much as you can even if your
health is impaired as it is likely to be at our age.
You still are concerned about cooking a meal for
a friend who is incapacitated. And how are you
going to deliver it? ... You know that can take a
hell of a lot of time to do. And it is a labour of
love. At the same time you are getting as much
out of it, or more, than you are giving.

Independence as a Life-Long Commitment

From their statements, it is clear that for these women, independence meant many things including being able to live
alone in their own homes, being able to get around the city
themselves, being able to express their own views on a particular subject, and being financially independent. A specific
theme relating to independence was that the women have
seen themselves as being independent throughout their
lives—when they were children, during their early adult
years, and as senior citizens. This theme is also expressed in
plans for independent futures.

In commenting on earlier periods of their lives, many of
the women reported that they have always been independent. As an eighty year old widow said:

So I learned independence at age eight ... as a
matter of fact, (my) independence may have
started at age eight, but (I) became very independent at age twelve.

On being independent from childhood, a seventy-seven year old married woman stated her early independence of thought by saying:

> When I was about twelve ... I decided that marriage was really bad, especially for women. And I read books and studied the mothers of my friends ... I was never going to get married.

This woman now has been married for almost fifty years, but the strength of her childhood memories, stated so clearly after all these years, indicates the level of independent thought that this woman remembered having had from childhood. This sentiment, expressed by others as well, gives insight into how these women see themselves as being independent seniors. They seem to be telling us that they consider themselves independent now as elderly women because they have always seen themselves as being independent. These statements can offer a new way to consider the complex question of how, or whether, elderly people learn social dependency in later life.[20]

In adulthood, most had worked outside the home throughout their lives. Given that these women are mostly in their mid-seventies, it is evident that they are markedly different from the majority of women in their age cohort since long-term participation in the paid labour force has not been a typical life course pattern for most elderly women—especially those who were married.[21] The independent behaviour of these women as adults reinforces the independence of thought that they remembered having had during their childhoods. It also completes the self-perception of these women of their independent status during their lifetime.

Throughout their lives, these women have also been interested in political issues. An eighty-seven year old single woman stated:

> I come from a family where, even as very young children, we talked a lot and discussed a lot at the table.

The women have consistently belonged to various local, provincial, and national environmental and social justice groups during their lives. Many were progressive thinkers and activists since their early adult years, interested in social change and social action. An eighty year old widow expressed her sentiments on this issue by stating:

> Left-wing women and men were the thinking persons. They saw during the Depression that we lived in a system which caused a great deal of poverty.

Two women were also very involved in organizing and setting up unions. A seventy-nine year old widow was involved in setting up a union in the educational system for teachers and an eighty-seven year old single woman was involved with unions in the textile industry. Through their involvement with various peace groups, as well as the VOW, it can be seen how these women have definitive views on world issues and demonstrate their independence in thought and action.

Given that many of the social and political interests with which these women were involved were those that they had participated in for many years, it was of interest to us to explore how they managed to balance their involvement with other activities. Many women stated that their parents had been strong independent role models, and that they learned independence skills from them. They stated that their mothers were especially supportive, but they also referred to the support that their fathers and siblings gave them in their pursuit of independence throughout their lives. Support often continued in their relationships with their spouses which helped the women maintain a level of commitment to these political activities. A seventy-nine year old widow, in discussing how she managed to maintain her life-long political interests at a time when there were major family demands on her time, introduced the idea of interdependence when she stated:

> And I had my interests. And he (her husband) always encouraged ... my having my own interests. So he would always stay with the kids, while I would run off to a meeting, or come home late for supper and he would have supper ready. It was real good co-operation.

In addition to telling us about how their independence developed during their childhoods and continued throughout their adult years, these women commented on aspects of independence in their lives as seniors. An important issue for these women was their living arrangements. For all of them, it was important to be able to live in their own homes as independently as possible and continue to do their shopping, cleaning, and cooking. Martin-Matthews reports that for elderly persons, independence is a highly valued goal realized through an ability to stay in comfortable surroundings, and that home is the place where things are familiar and where autonomy can be maintained. Thus, it becomes apparent, in general, that an elderly woman's housing situation is a critical indicator of her independence; in the case of the women we spoke to in this study, their current housing arrangements were also a major component of their perception of their present independence.

When discussing issues concerning their future, many of these women were again concerned with their living arrangements. All were strongly against going into a nursing home and wanted to remain in their own homes for as long as possible. Two women were so opposed to the idea of going into a nursing home that they considered suicide as an alternative. When asked what would happen if they could no longer live at home due to illness, one seventy-one year old separated woman replied:

> I would probably commit suicide because I am totally against these homes. I could never live there. Just the whole idea is totally foreign to me and it is against my principles. I would hope that

I would have the guts to just do away with myself.

A sixty-eight year old widow stated:

I would never go to a nursing home. Never. I wouldn't go into a senior citizen's residence either. Because I don't want to be with people of a certain age. I want to be with people. I want to be with children.

This generally negative reaction was tempered if the women thought they would be a burden on others, as in the following response from an eighty-one year old widow:

A nursing home! No. I wouldn't go into a nursing home. But if I were reduced in health to the point where I couldn't function, and where I was going to be a drag on somebody else, then I would consider a nursing home. I would consider that still a long way off.

Forbes et al. discuss the desire among elderly individuals to remain in familiar home settings and how they regard home as "independent living," whereas many elderly individuals have negative attitudes towards institutional settings and regard it as "dependent living."

To summarize this discussion on independence, these women stated that they had been independent from an early age and, with considerable support from significant others, had maintained this quality throughout their lives. They had worked both inside and outside the home, were interested in political issues and the VOW, had been involved with the formation of unions, were still able to maintain themselves independently in their own homes, and were firmly committed to retaining this independence as they aged.

Implications for Social Policy and Practice

This study of older, white, middle-class women points to the experiences of healthy independent elderly women and offers insight into how these women maintain their independence despite their reduced health resources which, in all cases, contributed to health problems. The wisdom that these women have shared with us has implications for social policy and practice in the field of gerontology in particular, and also in the area of the intergenerational sharing of independent thought by elderly women with women of younger generations.

The implications can be considered within a context of health realities and independence continuity. The recurring theme of functional health illustrates the health realities that elderly women must contend with on a daily basis. This certainly has implications for practitioners working with elderly women who will not be able to achieve the abstract level of ideal health as defined by policy makers. Many practitioners such as nurses, doctors, social workers, community workers, and physical and occupational therapists in community settings do, in fact, work with seniors to define and achieve a level of functional health that will allow them to maintain as much independence as possible. This work must continue to be supported because this is the level of health which, as this study indicated, most seniors will accept in the more likely absence of complete health. These women are aware that the abstract level of health touted by policy makers and supported by the proponents of the medical model approach to health is not attainable.

The health-related comments of these women also raise a question that can be addressed by policy analysts. Based on the often-repeated statement that these women were operating on a functional level of health, the question can be asked: Should elderly women (or elderly people, in general) have a different definition of health from that of a "state of complete physical, mental and social well-being" that others are meant to achieve? If the answer to this question is "yes," then it assumes a two-tiered level of health at the policy and the practice level. This would not be acceptable in the Canadian context, which promotes the "health for all" philosophy. The answer must then be "no."

This conclusion, in concert with the theme of functional health that the VOW women highlighted in this study, must lead to a reevaluation of health policy that promotes a level of unattainable health for a significant proportion (if not all) of the population. We would argue, based on what these active older women told us about their health realities, that a policy statement on health should reflect a more realistic definition of a level of health that would encompass the theme of "health for all" in both spirit and practice for the whole population. This statement could focus on a continuum of health that acknowledges that health is flexible throughout the life cycle, in that there are different levels of health at different times in each person's life.

If, as we would argue, this new statement were to be based on the theme of functional health as indicated by the women we interviewed, there would have to be a related shift in health resources to increase the social support component of health care that elderly people, among others, need, more than the technical interventions that are often promoted as the significant aspects of a modern health care system. This is not to say that technical interventions are unimportant to health care; it is only to say that, based on what these healthy elderly women told us, it is important to support the concept of functional health while the ever-present, and arguably unreasonable, search for complete health is pursued. In effect, we must not neglect the present users of the health care system in the interests of providing future generations with the unrealistic goal of complete health.

A conclusion related to independence that we can draw from the responses obtained, is that independence in later life is linked to continuity. That is, these women told us that they were independent in later life because they were independent throughout their lives. This kind of continuity of perception and behaviour is what Atchley describes as internal continuity which allows an individual to make links with the past in meaningful ways.[22] Given that these women developed a sense of independence during an era that is not generally seen as one in which this characteristic was actively promoted for women, we can learn a considerable amount about how to influence social policy and practice in the promotion of independence of elderly women from what they had to say.

The views that these ten older women from the Voice of Women presented to us are very useful in providing some guidelines about how to develop and maintain independence in later life. Their thoughts can also be considered in order to give a sense of reality to some of the theoretical statements that are made by researchers, practitioners and policy makers about life in old age. The issue of independence as a continuous activity should be placed in the context of internal and external continuity as discussed by Atchley. External continuity is a concept defined as "a remembered structure of physical and social environments, role relationships, and activities."[23] Perceptions of external continuity result from being in familiar environments, practising familiar skills, and interacting with familiar people. Most women in this study had been involved with the VOW for twenty-five to thirty years. Thus, not only is the group familiar to them but the social relationships it has created, which have been consistent over the years, have helped them adjust to old age and to maintain their independence. Atchley states that, "like familiar activities and thought, the company of familiar people provides a sense of one's individual identity and allows for a sense of belonging."[24] It is evident then, that involvement with the VOW over the years has helped these women maintain an important link with an earlier period of their lives and, therefore, maintain internal continuity as older women in their sense of independence.

Social workers involved in planning social and health care services for elderly women could bear in mind the importance of continuity in elderly women's lives. Because many elderly women are widowed with decreased social support, social workers can link them with organizations or groups that were formerly of interest to them as a way of encouraging them to keep active in personal interests. In a study by Gass, widows dealt with the loss of their spouses by returning to diverse individual, social or political activities they had had little time for when their spouse was ill. These activities helped widows regain the sense of independence they had voluntarily given up for a period of time. The study reinforces the notion of a flexible continuum of independence that many elderly women experience in later life if they are involved in informal caregiving tasks.

The women in our study received many benefits from their association with the VOW. They find that it helps them to maintain their independence by being able to express their views on issues of importance and by being able to share these views with other like-minded women. Their involvement with the VOW also contributes to their sense of self-esteem, since they belong to a group where their presence is needed, and by their collective voice they can contribute to social change in the world. Also, their involvement with the VOW means that they keep busy working on issues of peace and, as they have said to us, have less time to worry about their own health. As well as benefiting personally from their activities and interests, these women also contribute much to the many groups to which they belong. Due to the wisdom they have achieved through a lifetime of varied experiences, they are valuable resources for the VOW, as well as for other groups.

Such women can act as educators to help everyone learn about independence in later life. Frances Barskey is an example of a senior acting in an educating role. She has been a senior consultant in a course on aging in the School of Social Work at McGill University for seven years. She attends each class to provide information about what it is really like to be an eighty year old woman living in Montréal in the 1990s. This information bridges the gap between theory and the reality of aging by conveying experiences of a healthy, independent elderly woman to students who will soon be entering the field of social work. Other such women could also be resources for similar activities, such as speaking to social workers who work in hospitals, nursing homes, or community health centres. Social workers could locate elderly women who have been teachers, nurses, homemakers, businesswomen, farmworkers, factory workers or others, in order to channel their knowledge and experience into educating younger people in the community about what it is like to be an independent, healthy elderly female and how to maintain this independence despite declining physical health.

Since social policy analysts are interested in the promotion of independence of women in retirement or later life, it is important to consider the views of the elderly women in this study. Women who are healthy and independent in old age could be engaged as consultants in the many settings in which there are young females to talk to about how they developed their sense of independence, for example, schools, play schools, religious organizations, girl guides, sports groups, universities and many others.

By linking healthy, independent elderly women with young girls and adolescent females in search of ways to develop and maintain independence throughout a lifetime, an intergenerational transfer of independence skills and thought for women and girls could be developed. This activity would contribute to the maintenance of the independence of elderly women and to the development of independence of succeeding generations of females. This is such an important contribution to the increasing development of society that social policy could promote supplementing much of the informal work that is already going on in this domain.

It is clear from this study that the elderly women we interviewed have very strong ideas about the concept of independence for women in later life. However, despite the fact that this sample of healthy independent elderly women is a very small group, it can be expected that there are many other women over the age of sixty-five who would also consider themselves healthy and independent. As the ten women from the Voice of Women conveyed a marvellous sense of health and independence, so too could many other elderly women convey the same sense of these two important and socially-desired characteristics if they had an opportunity to define their own level of health and independence. It seems to us that there is a significant and untapped source of information and inspiration in most Canadian communities. It simply requires the ability to perceive the vast majority of elderly women as they perceive themselves, and asking them how they managed to achieve this high level of functional health and independence.

Conclusion

The elderly women in this study have shown through their comments the importance of maintaining their health and independence. As with the majority of their age cohort, these women are experiencing a decline in health, however, through their involvement with the VOW, and their concerns for environmental and social justice issues, they lead active lives and are not preoccupied with limitations related to their health problems. Also, for these ten elderly women from the VOW, independence was learned and practised at an early age, continued throughout their lives, and now allows them to meet the challenges of the present and the future. Social work practitioners and policy analysts in the field of gerontology would benefit from the views and experiences of these elderly women to reflect on their practice and programme development with seniors.

Notes

1. Marshall 1987; Meigs 1991.
2. Baines, Evans and Neysmith 1991; Kay and Applegate 1990; Forbes and MacLean 1989.
3. Chappel, Strain and Blandford 1986.
4. Devereaux, 1991.
5. Gass 1987.
6. Martin-Matthews 1987.
7. Walker 1982.
8. Gee and Kimball 1987.
9. Health and Welfare Canada 1986, p. 3.
10. Gee and Kimball 1987.
11. Ibid.
12. Black 1985.
13. Thomas 1985.
14. Wister and Strain 1986; Chappell 1983.
15. Martin-Matthews 1989.
16. Kalish 1975.
17. Martin-Matthews 1987.
18. Lowy 1989.
19. Aronson 1992; Wilkin and Hughes 1987.
20. Heppner, Leonard, MacLean, Marcus and Woodsworth 1988.
21. Martin-Matthews 1989; Wister and Strain 1988.
22. Atchley 1989.
23. Ibid., p. 189.
24. Ibid.

References

Aronson, J. (1992). Are We Really Listening? Beyond the Official Discourse on Needs of Old People. *Canadian Social Work Review.*

Atchley, R.C. (1989). "A Continuity Theory of Normal Aging." *The Gerontologist,* 29(1), 183-190.

Baines, C., Evans, P. and Neysmith, S. (eds.) (1991). *Women's Caring: Feminist Perspectives on Social Welfare.* Toronto: McClelland and Stewart, Inc.

Black, M. (1985). Health and Social Support of Older Adults in the Community. *Canadian Journal on Aging,* 4(4), 213-226.

Chappell, N.L. (1983). "Informal Support Networks Among the Elderly." *Research On Aging,* 5(1), 77-99.

Devereaux, M.S. (1991). Personal Communication. Ottawa: Statistics Canada.

Forbes, W.F., Jackson, J.A., and Kraus, A.S. (1987). *Institutionalization of the Elderly in Canada.* Toronto: Butterworths.

Forbes, W.F. and MacLean, M.J. (1989). *An Examination of Innovative Approaches by Public Health, Health Services and Social Services to Address Seniors' Independence.* Ottawa: Health and Welfare, Canada.

Gass, K.A. (1987). "The Health of Conjugally Bereaved Older Widows: The Role of Appraisal, Coping and Resources." *Research in Nursing and Health,* 10(1): 39-47.

Gee, E.M., and Kimball, M.M. (1987). *Women and Aging.* Toronto: Butterworths.

Health and Welfare Canada (1986). *Achieving Health for All: A Framework for Health Promotion.* Ottawa: Health and Welfare, Canada.

Heppner, B., Leonard, P., MacLean, M., Marcus, L. and Woodsworth, D. (1988). "Learning Social Dependency in Old Age." Paper Presented at *Connections '88: International Conference on Research in Health and Aging.* Saskatoon, February.

Kallish, R.A. (1975). *Late Adulthood: Perspective on Human Development.* Monterey, CA: Brooks-Cole Publishing Company.

Kaye, L. and Applegate, G. (1990). *Men as Caregivers to the Elderly: Understanding and Aiding Unrecognized Family Support.* Lexington, MA: Lexington Books.

Lowy, L. (1989). "Independence and Dependence in Aging: A New Balance." *Journal of Gerontological Social Work.* 13(3/4), 133-146.

Marshall, D. (1987). *Silver Threads: Critical Reflections on Growing Old.* Toronto: Between the Lines Press.

Martin-Matthews, A. (1989). *Contributors to the Loss of Independence and Promotion of Independence Among Seniors.* Ottawa. Health and Welfare, Canada.

Martin-Matthews, A. (1987). "Widowhood as an Expectable Life Event." In V.W. Marshall (Ed.), *Aging in Canada: Social Perspectives,* (2nd ed.), (pp. 343-366). Toronto: Fitzhenry and Whiteside.

Meigs, M. (1991). *In The Company of Strangers.* Vancouver: Talon Books.

Thomas, P.D., Garry, P.J., Goodwin, J.M., and Goodwin, J.S. (1985). "Social Bonds in a Healthy Elderly Sample: Characteristics and Associated Variable." *Social Science Medical,* 20(4), 356-369.

Walker, A. (1982). "Dependency and Old Age." *Social Policy and Administration.* 16(2), 115-135.

Wilkin, D. and Hughes, B. (1987). "Residential Care of Elderly People: The Consumer's Views." *Aging and Society,* 7, 175-201.

Wister, A.V. and Strain, L. (1986). "Social Support and Well-being: A Comparison of Older Widows and Widowers." *Canadian Journal on Aging,* 5(3), 205-219.

5

A View From the Other Side

David Woodsworth

When I was talking with another retired professor, she expressed feelings almost identical to my own about retirement when she said "It's like getting out of a box." Probably each person has her own "box," and for many, men perhaps more than women, retirement isn't so much an experience of freedom as of threat, of being cast adrift onto an unknown sea. But for me it has been a release, and this paper is a personal report of my own experience of retirement which may have some meaning for others, both old and young.

I must begin by talking about myself in the first-person. This is somewhat improper because it sets modesty aside; besides, it transgresses the rules of academia and of professionalism, which require things to be expressed impersonally, as if they were above personal concerns. But that, of course, is a fiction in most academic and professional work.

I am, first, a man. For the last ten years or so I have been trying to understand the feminist position, but it is only since retiring that I think I am beginning to get the idea, mostly because retirement goes a long way in removing both the advantages and the compulsions of male status. One of my boxes has been being a man, but it is less rigid than it was.

Second, I have been relatively "successful" in the external world. Almost all of my working life, I have been in some kind of position of authority over others—as a manager of professional or educational organizations, or as a professor. These jobs have also brought modest economic success—not enough to make me "rich," but still enough to put me, with many other professionals, in the top 10 percent range of incomes, and therefore to bring me respected social status. Three boxes are involved here, defined in terms of: professional attitudes; managerial attitudes and power; and the affluence related to both. These are the boxes into which most people are trying to put themselves because, of course, they bring various gratifications, but like other social boxes, they separate a person from other potential relationships. I have, thankfully, been partly liberated from some of them.

Third, I was born into a Methodist missionary family. This created some guidelines for my development and self-identification, three being predominant. The first was that religion, as belief and as observance, was a help rather than a hindrance to understanding the purpose of life. The second was a radical, even revolutionary view of my own rights and responsibilities: I had a right and a responsibility to tell right from wrong, and to do something about it. And third was a recognition of the diversity of the world's peoples and of their commonality as human beings.

For a long time then, I have lived in a kind of tension. On the one hand, experienced in the first two types of boxes, was the desire and obligation to do my best in the world and to use whatever status and power I had to good purpose; and on the other, in the third box, was an impatience with the existing state of affairs, and a need to change it. From the second point of view, the first was a false road to follow, and I never felt entirely comfortable or legitimate in my work roles. It was as if I was pretending to be someone else. Retirement has relieved me to some extent of the first set of demands, and has allowed me to behave more fully in the framework of the second. I think I may have been experiencing Marx's notion of alienation in work: the work didn't really belong to me, because I was usually doing it for some external authority. Now it does.

I also relate to Northrop Frye's distinction between myths of *concern* and myths of *freedom*. Of course Frye doesn't use the word "myth" in a negative way, rather, he uses it to indicate systems of meaning. In effect, concern offers a focus in meaning and purpose—and this is typical of both academic and professional work, as it is of various religious and political positions. Concerns are essential for human survival, and offer the starting point for change—or revolution. But Frye points out that as they are institutionalized, concerns become "closed"; they must justify themselves, right or wrong, and they do this by their own internal standards. Freedom, on the other hand, is freedom of the imagination, freedom to consider other possibilities. Neither of these positions can do without the other; they are effectively stages that create continuing tension. (Frye's ideas are expressed in many of his books, for example in *The Critical Path; An Essay on the Social*

Context of Literary Criticism.) In a sense, we can't do without boxes, but we can't afford to trust them for too long.

These ideas need some elaboration. Certain aspects of the modern world may represent its major "concern": its predominant beliefs support goal achievement and precision of thought in terms of quantification and objectification. These are beliefs in the power of rationality to solve problems and the devaluation of non-rational—often called irrational—thinking and behaviour. They have been used to justify the centralization of power and control of society, even though they very often fail to be what they claim to be, or to achieve what they claim to achieve. But they do manage to prevent the exercise of imagination which encourages deviation from accepted patterns of thought. This is obvious in centres of government and in large organizations and corporations.

The values of rationality are familiar enough to social workers and social work students and educators. They are increasingly used to define the authority of social work agencies and the role of social workers, restricting both in their efforts to do what professional values would require. Social workers are always being called upon to contain the irrationalities of their clients—considered irrational by the State, that is. In academic life too, there are formalities that emphasize intellectual precision. Specialization, to whatever degree, means discipline, which refers to the ability to think and work in a specified field, without reference to other knowledge. This is of course inevitable in a world where knowledge far exceeds a person's ability to grasp it, but the consequences are that as the management of society becomes ever more complex, individuals have fewer opportunities for a more diverse understanding.

In social work, as in some other professions and also in established churches, there is a division between people whose "concern" is with the inner dimensions of the human condition—psychological, spiritual—and those whose concern is with the social and physical environment. Both give some recognition to the other, but specialization exacts its costs. Even within these groups, there are subdivisions. Behaviourists differ from Freudians; systems theorists differ from Marxists; and furthermore, there are sub-subdivisions within each of these. What happens eventually is that people in these subdivisions lose the capacity and even the wish to communicate at depth with others. The divisions are then no longer just intellectual separations; they spill over into the emotional lives of the proponents, and into battles for power, because it is through such battles that people win or lose their right to continue their specializing processes.

Frye argues that the university is essential to modern society because it can keep open the idea of freedom and creative thought. And so it should; but he perhaps underestimates the ways in which concerns within the university also become closed. The pressures are strong on a young teacher to "produce," that is, to do research and to publish in an area of specialization. Over time, that tends to foster the development of old professors with fixed and limited concerns. And university administrators are of course not immune to all this; they are bound to support the myth.

Another difficulty for universities is that they are increasingly seen as instruments of the State and as producers of technicians for the specialized society: they are not expected to produce critics of that society. Social workers are familiar with this situation; as professionals they are "concerned" with the welfare of their clients, what is to be done with them, and how, but there is little freedom of imagination involved.

These are some of the boxes in which I have felt contained as a social worker, professor, and administrator. As a man, I have both benefited from them and been constrained by them, because men tend to be given the opportunities to acquire authority and status, and are therefore compelled to fulfil the myths. As women acquire equal status with men, they too are subjected to these same forms of servitude.

All of this is not to say that people have ever been, or should ever be free of social obligations. I am not a flower child. On the contrary, I think it is only through deep commitment to others that one can find fulfilment of the self. My complaint concerns two other issues. The first involves the tyranny of closed concerns. I think that throughout history there has been a need to oppose the "powers that be" simply because they would not be powerful if they did not already exclude competing ideas. The second is about the specific nature of the modern concern as I summarized it above. The effort to introduce "rationality" into the management of human affairs is, to say the least, premature. We behave as if scientific thought could be transferred to the examination of social problems, but nobody really understands the complexity of those problems so "solutions" are based on partial and underdeveloped concepts. In any case, rational and scientific methods are not really used by administrators; there is just a pretence of doing so. Usually this pretence masks goals and attitudes that are highly emotional. The only way to counter this situation is to allow for imagination and deviance, even within accepted social obligations.

On the other side of my history—the Methodist missionary side—there is much to be explained to those who are unfamiliar with Methodism. Suffice to say, perhaps, that Methodism began as an eighteenth-century rebellion against perceived corruption in older churches. It did of course quickly develop its own rigidity, but a commitment to social change has continued to this day. It also offered its adherents the notion that morality was each his or her own responsibility. This has led to extremes in interpretation in both right- and left-wing politics, but despite these distortions, the commonly accepted principle is that of personal responsibility. It is clear that this principle not only allows me, but requires me to take action "by my own lights" though this must be done in a framework of rules, one of which is the respect of others. Their rights and responsibilities allow for mine. Of course when there are competing "others," I have to decide which I am to side with—a decision demanding freedom of imagination.

For me, retirement has partly removed the status of professor and social worker, and certainly that of administrator. But it has left me with the knowledge and abilities that I had before, and can dispose of as I will within the limits of my rules of morality. The more time passes since my departure from my former job, the less chance there is that people will know me through my profession so that I can begin to be accepted (or rejected) for what I do and say rather than for my position in society. This is a considerable relief.

One of the main things I have done is been myself: that is, I have been an old man. As such, I have taken an active part in developing an organization for "seniors." Here I can be accepted as a member of the group without any pretence or disguise. Although I am not as poor as most seniors, all seniors (or all who allow themselves contact with others) experience relative loss of status and the threat of a loss of dignity and respect. There is, in this, a kind of common bond that encourages us to help each other; it is a bond that goes beyond at least some of the divisions of gender, class, and ethnicity. We recognize each other as brothers and sisters. After a lifetime of professional detachment, of academic detachment, and of class estrangement, this is a major gift.

One of the things that characterizes old people as a group is that most of them are women, and this is true of seniors' organizations. The group I work with is not only run for women; it is also largely run by women, both as staff and as volunteers. And since it is an organization of and for seniors, it is not especially guided by the usual rituals of organizational procedure. True, it has to meet the expectations of funding sources, but these don't usually require disclosure of the real treatment of receivers and are easily satisfied. Fortunately, we have as treasurer a man whose life was spent meeting such expectations, so he knows how to deal with them. Other than that, the rules are internal and can be used to fit women's standards.

As a man then, I have benefited from the chance to learn how to relate to people rather than to rules as such, and my emotional life has expanded greatly as a result. I have not been entirely free of the male role because I still possess abilities that can be used for the group, but I no longer feel that others' success depends on me. Success, in fact, is not for me to define. I act as an instrument of the group, as far as I can be aware of it, and I learn from it. Besides, the women are willing to let me do what I can to help and their acceptance is a blessing. The result is that my life has been enriched far more than it was during decades of professional life.

Part of letting go of the burden of the male role is the change in one's perception of time. When one is in a job there is always a deadline. There is also an awareness of a lifetime trajectory which starts when you are a small child, when people say "What do you want to be when you grow up?" As you get older, you check yourself against your own aspirations and against the achievements of others; that's the nature of a competitive society. But when you are old, these pressures tend to melt away. There is, in fact, no predictable future. You are aware that all you hold dear may disappear in hours or days; you may yourself die at any time. What you can achieve, then, tends to be valued for what it is, as much as for what it may lead to. It is this enriched way of experiencing life that my senior women have helped me to understand.

Let me give an example. I do some volunteer driving which includes picking up older people and driving them to various destinations. When I arrive at one "foster home," I see that the interior is dark and threadbare. There doesn't seem to be much help available for the woman I am there to pick up as she shuffles along. I help her step by step down the front stairs and walk to my car as she holds tight to my arm. I am aware of her fragility, and I hope she is aware of my comparative strength and the warmth of my body. Then, because I am a bit worried about her, I ask how she likes the foster home. She surprises me with her appreciation and approval; she says they are so kind, so good. She asks if I will be driving her home again. The next time I drive her, she remarks that she is walking better and she makes a few comments on what she sees out the car window. Well, in short, I am beginning to make a friend and I remember my experience as enriching and human. I think I might have felt that way as a practising social worker; in fact I remember similar relationships, although they were not "professional," but personal. Part of being a social worker involves putting yourself into the relationship, but it is precisely that aspect of it that seems to be increasingly denied by the institutionalizing processes we are going through. In my present role as an old man volunteer, I can enjoy the luxury of being myself.

All of this may look like an idealization of what is often a painful, boring, and attenuated approach to death, and I don't want to appear ignorant of that side of things. Not long ago, I saw an old friend die over a period of months, with a progressive loss of his awareness and his dignity. But that was when he was eighty-five, after years of positive and active retirement. There are people who die before their death, and many who are forced into that state by the boxes imposed by professional and bureaucratic rules. I can only say that as a senior I can resist that imposition, and should do so, because this is the only time in my life that I can do it, when the choices are simplified.

Being a senior has helped me in another area as well. There is a great deal in common between seniors and poor people, especially people on welfare. Both groups are outside the labour market and are accordingly devalued. I have, as a senior, been accepted as a member of a group of welfare recipients, even though they know I am not on welfare and am "middle-class." They accept me because I am a senior, and they know what we have in common. It has been a source of pleasure to be accepted and to be able to offer my skills to the group, although the sense of unity is not as strong as it is with seniors, since people on welfare are still hoping to somehow "make it." The fact that I have learned, to some extent, not to expect to "make it" has made me able to accept the uncertain and slow pace of change in the poor people's group. I can share their anger about what happens to them but I don't have to feel personally defeated by it, so I can be more patient. This, I have learned as a senior.

This same sense of patience, if that's what it is, also makes me less despairing about public policy. Not that I am less critical or pessimistic about the behaviour of politicians and bureaucrats; if anything, I feel more able to see through them and to despise their pretences, and I deeply resent their lies and their manipulation. I am also free to criticize them more directly and openly than before because I no longer have institutional concerns to worry about. But perhaps I expect less of politicians now; they are less important to my sense of the world, or at least what my own life is about. I can, with more patience, look forward to the time when they will be gone, or when I will be gone.

Anyone who watches the news on television, with its focus on the posturing of our politicians, or, just as bad, with its "expert" commentaries by journalists whose ideas, put forward with such certainty, have been thought up during the preceding hour or two, must be aware that it is unlikely that our government will be able to solve our problems. Their rationality is not up to it. It seems likely though, that we will move either toward a totalitarian form of government where central decisions are enforced, or to a very decentralized form with inadequate co-ordination of activities. Of the two, I prefer the latter, though the former seems more likely in the immediate future. But perhaps this dichotomy is exaggerated, and instead we may find multiple solutions.

For the time being, one of the advantages I have had as a senior is to be a member of the Quebec Coalition of Seniors. Here French and English speaking people meet in the spirit of shared concern. Conversations are in both languages and if people don't understand, someone takes the trouble to explain. We are united in our attitudes about the needs of seniors, and these are more important than language. So big public debates about Meech Lake or the referendum, for example, are unimportant to us. This is a sort of prototype of the kind of governing processes we might anticipate. I think a fair analogy might be exploratory voyages, to the North and

South Poles for example. It was found that expeditions carrying too much equipment resulted in death, while those that travelled light succeeded. Seniors have ditched a lot of baggage. Though it may be Utopian to think that the seniors' way of thinking might be applied to political and economic realities, it is a good model. In the meantime, becoming and being a senior has been a wonderful experience that I wish for you all.

RETHINKING CAMELOT
JFK, the Vietnam War, and U.S. Political Culture
Noam Chomsky

A thorough analysis of John F. Kennedy's role in the U.S. invasion of Vietnam and a probing reflection on the elite political culture that allowed and encouraged the Cold War. Chomsky dismisses efforts to resurrect Camelot — an attractive American myth portraying JFK as a shining knight promising peace. Contrary to prominent figures such as Oliver Stone (director of *JFK*), historian Arthur Schlesinger, and John Newman (author of *JFK and Vietnam*), Chomsky argues that U.S. institutions and political culture, not individual presidents, are the key to understanding U.S. behaviour during the Vietnam War.

200 pages, index
Paperback ISBN: 1-895431-72-7 $19.95
Hardcover ISBN: 1-895431-73-5 $38.95

GLOBAL VISIONS
Beyond the New World Order
Jeremy Brecher, John Brown Childs, and Jill Culter, editors

All over the world, grassroots movements are forging links across national boundaries to resist the New World Order. Their aims are to restore the power of communities to nurture their environments; to enhance the access of ordinary people to the resources they need; and to democratize local, national, and international institutions. Such efforts provide a practical starting point for the construction of a genuine world community. *Global Visions* initiates a crucial worldwide discussion on what such an alternative might be — and on how to create it.

The contributors are scholars and activists associated with environmental, peace, labour, women's, human rights, development, and democracy movements in more than twenty countries on five continents. They include Vandana Shiva, the late Petra Kelly, Martin Khor, Cuauhtémoc Cárdenas, Denis MacShane, Saskia Sassen, Muto Ikhiyo, Elise Boulding, Haunani-Kay Trask, Richard Falk, Hassan Sunmonu, Elaine Bernard, Lula, Francis M. Deng, and many others.

320 pages
Paperback ISBN: 1-895431-74-3 $19.95
Hardcover ISBN: 1-895431-75-1 $38.95

POLITICAL ECOLOGY
Beyond Environmentalism
Dimitrios I. Roussopoulos

Examining the perspective offered by various components of political ecology, this book presents an overview of its origins as well as its social and cultural causes. It summarizes the differences, and similarities, between political ecology and social ecology, while revealing, quite candidly, that the resolution of the present planetary crisis hinges on the outcome and consequences of this new politics.

Contents include: The Ecological Challenge, Intellectual Flirtations, The State Management of the Environment, Transnational Ecologists, What Perspectives and What Politics?

180 pages
Paperback ISBN: 1-895431-80-8 $15.95
Hardcover ISBN: 1-895431-81-6 $34.95

RACE, GENDER AND WORK
A Multi-Cultural Economic History of Women in the United States
Teresa Amott and Julie Matthaei

Race, Gender, and Work traces women's work lives through the dynamic and complicated process which economists have called capitalist development. It uncovers the multiplicity and diversity of women's work contributions, both paid and unpaid, to our economic history.

Race, Gender, and Work is exciting because of its frank acknowledgement of difference among women. It is a volume that will inform and motivate scholars and activists.
Julianne Malveaux, University of California, Berkeley

...a detailed, richly textured history of American working women.
Barbara Ehrenreich, author of The Worst Years of Our Lives

433 pages, index, appendices
Paperback ISBN: 0-921689-90-X $19.95
Hardcover ISBN: 0-921689-91-8 $38.95

BUREAUCRACY AND COMMUNITY
Linda Davies and Eric Shragge, editors

...takes a highly critical view of social-services management and the controlling role of government bureaucracies.
Calgary Herald

180 pages, bibliography
Paperback ISBN: 0-920057-56-X $16.95
Hardcover ISBN: 0-920057-57-8 $35.95
L.C. No. 90-81638